Who Jesus Was

Other titles by Avril Rowlands

All the Tales from the Ark

*The Animals' Caravan: The Journey Begins
**The Animals' Caravan: Stories Jesus Told
***The Animals' Caravan: The Journey Continues

Look out for this symbol*. You will find these stories in the earlier books in the series.

The Animals' Caravan

Who Jesus Was

Adventures through the Bible
with Caravan Bear and friends

Avril Rowlands
Illustrated by Kay Widdowson

LION
CHILDREN'S

To Nick Wright
With my love and thanks for your friendship and help. A. R.

Text copyright © 2020 Avril Rowlands
Illustrations copyright © 2020 Kay Widdowson
This edition copyright © 2020 Lion Hudson IP Limited

The right of Avril Rowlands to be identified as the author and of Kay Widdowson to be identified as the illustrator of this work has been asserted by them in accordance with the Copyright, Designs and Patents Act 1988.

All rights reserved. No part of this publication may be reproduced or transmitted in any form or by any means, electronic or mechanical, including photocopy, recording, or any information storage and retrieval system, without permission in writing from the publisher.

Published by
Lion Hudson Limited
Wilkinson House, Jordan Hill Business Park,
Banbury Road, Oxford OX2 8DR, England
www.lionhudson.com

ISBN 978 0 7459 7813 0
eISBN 978 0 7459 7814 7

First edition 2020

A catalogue record for this book is available from the British Library

Printed and bound in the UK, December 2019, LH26

Contents

1. Star in the East *Matthew 2* — 07
2. Jesus in the Temple *Luke 2* — 22
3. Jesus is Baptized *Matthew 3* — 40
4. In the Wilderness *Matthew 4; Luke 4* — 52
5. Jesus in Jerusalem *Matthew 21; Mark 11; Luke 19* — 71
6. The Last Supper *Matthew 26; Mark 14; Luke 22; John 13* — 87
7. In the Garden *Matthew 26–27; Mark 14–15; Luke 22–23* — 104
8. The Empty Tomb *Matthew 27–28; Luke 23–24; John 20* — 124

1

Star in the East

"This is the life!" said Whitby the dog, bouncing up and down the steps of the caravan.

"Careful!" warned Caravan Bear as he was almost pushed off.

"But it is, isn't it?" Whitby went on. "Off on our adventures – here, there…"

"…wherever the fancy takes us!" added Caravan Bear, Hector the horse, and Christopher Rabbit.

Caravan Bear began to sing and the others joined in.

"Clip clop, clip clop.
Travelling fast or travelling slow,
Look very hard and you might see it go:
The bright caravan on the road.
Clip clop, clip clop.
Caravan Bear and all of his friends,
Hector and Whitby, and Rabbit as well,

*Off for adventure, off for some fun,
Off for adventure, out in the sun.
Clip clop, clip clop, clip clip clop."*

The caravan journeyed on, its wheels turning busily on the road.

They climbed higher and higher until they reached wide, open moorland. For once, even Hector didn't grumble as he puffed and panted, towing the heavy caravan. The scenery around them was so beautiful.

They stopped late in the afternoon, as the sun was just beginning to dip low on the horizon.

As it was a warm evening, they had supper sitting outside. When they had eaten, they watched the sun go down and turn the sky brilliant shades of red and gold.

Caravan Bear stretched himself lazily. "What a lovely start to our holiday."

He glanced at his caravan. He had only finished repainting it the other day before packing it with the things needed for their summer adventure. The caravan's bright-red body and yellow wheels gleamed. Caravan Bear nodded. It looked good, he thought. It looked very good.

Christopher Rabbit lay back and looked up at the wide blue sky arching high above him. A skylark flew toward a clump of trees in the far distance. He continued to watch as the sky changed to a deeper blue and the first star of evening appeared. He sniffed. The air smelled of warm, growing things.

Whitby ran round and round the caravan, her tail waving wildly, a big smile on her face.

Hector, having had a good meal of oats and two carrots, grunted. "Bit better than that time when the wheel came off the caravan. Do you remember?"**

"And we had to take shelter in a stable," Whitby added, coming to sit on the steps.

"Barn," Hector corrected. "The cows didn't like it being called a stable."

"And I read the story about Jesus being born in a stable," Christopher Rabbit added.

"Or barn," said Hector, grinning.

"Oh, stop being difficult, Hector," Whitby said. "It says 'stable' in the Bible, doesn't it, Christopher Rabbit?"

"I'm not sure," said Christopher Rabbit. "Wait a minute and I'll check."

He went inside the caravan and returned with his Bible.

Christopher Rabbit's Bible was very important to him. He had found it on his birthday. He had organized a party, but no one had come. He later found out that he had forgotten to post any invitations but at the time he had been very upset. He had run out of his house in search of his friends and had fallen over a brightly wrapped parcel on the road outside his front gate. It had been addressed to him and inside had been a big book – the Bible.

At that moment a caravan had come hurtling down the road and he had been sure he would be run over. But it had stopped just in time and Caravan Bear, Whitby, and Hector had asked him to join them. A spring and a summer of wonderful adventures had followed.

Christopher Rabbit carried his Bible on every journey and read stories from it to the other animals.

He opened the book and found the right place. "It actually says 'manger', not stable or barn," he said.

"A manger is a sort of trough where farmers put the animals' food, isn't it?" asked Whitby.

"So the baby could have been put in a manger in a barn," Hector said smugly.

"Oh, do be quiet!" Whitby retorted.

"Didn't the shepherds bring their sheep to say hello to the baby?" asked Caravan Bear.

"I expect so," agreed Christopher Rabbit.

"Did anyone else visit Jesus?" Hector asked.

Christopher Rabbit turned the page, but it was getting dark and quite hard to read. Caravan Bear fetched an oil lamp. He lit it and hung it on a stick, which he stuck into the ground. Whitby and Hector drew nearer.

"Some wise men had heard about the birth of Jesus," Christopher Rabbit said. "They wanted to see him…"

"Why?" asked Hector

"Why what?"

"Why did they want to see him? I mean, one baby is pretty much like another, I'd have thought."

"This was a *special* baby," Whitby insisted.

"He was God's own son," Caravan Bear explained.

"The wise men had seen a new star, which had risen in the east, and they had heard that a new king, the king of the Jews, had been born," Christopher Rabbit explained. "They came from a different country, many miles away from Bethlehem. They decided to follow the star, so they set off on a long journey across the desert."

Hector, always interested in how people and animals got around, asked, "How did they travel? On horseback?"

"Probably not," Christopher Rabbit said. "I expect they rode on camels."

"Oh, camels!" said Hector, scornfully. "Horses would have been faster."

"I've never seen a camel," said Whitby. "Why do people ride them?"

"Because they can go for miles across the desert without needing water," Christopher Rabbit replied.

"Makes me thirsty," said Whitby.

Caravan Bear went into the caravan to get drinks.

"How many wise men were there?" asked Whitby when Caravan Bear returned.

"It doesn't say in the Bible," said Christopher Rabbit.

"Three," said Caravan Bear. "That's what I heard. And I thought they were kings."

"They might have been kings," Christopher Rabbit agreed.

"Although not all kings are wise, are they? They've been very stupid in some of the stories you've told us," replied Hector.

"And their names were – " Caravan Bear continued.

"Caspar, Balthasar, and Melchior," interrupted Hector .

"It doesn't say that in the Bible either," said Christopher Rabbit .

"How do you know their names?" asked Whitby curiously.

Hector shrugged. "I know a lot more than you think."

"I never thought you stupid," said Whitby, kindly.

"Thank you," Hector replied and began nibbling the grass. He was feeling a little hungry even after the large meal he had just eaten.

Who Jesus Was

"Shall I go on?" asked Christopher Rabbit, moving the lamp so it shone more directly on the Bible. It was almost dark now.

"Please do," said Caravan Bear.

"The king at that time was a man called Herod. When the wise men arrived at his palace in Jerusalem, they asked King Herod where they could find the baby who, they said, was born to be King of the Jews. They told him about the special, brilliant star and said…"

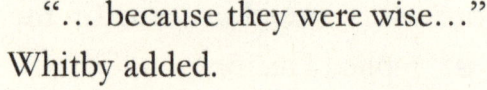

"… because they were wise…" Whitby added.

"… that this wasn't any ordinary star – it was a star that would lead them to the baby."

"So why did they bother going to Jerusalem to ask the king?" asked Caravan Bear. "All they had to do was follow the star."

"Perhaps they were just being polite," said Hector. "They might have thought that they shouldn't travel through King Herod's land without paying their respects."

"And they might have thought that if a king had been born, it would be in somewhere grand like a palace, not a stable," Christopher Rabbit said. "Or barn," he added.

Whitby wrinkled her nose. "Wasn't it odd for Jesus, God's son and King of the Jews, to be born in a stable? Bit of a smelly place."

"Especially when the shepherds and their sheep arrived," Hector added.

"Do you think God was making a point – that Jesus was born for everyone, not just for kings and rich people?" Caravan Bear asked.

Christopher Rabbit nodded. "I expect so. Anyway, the wise men told King Herod that they wanted to find the child and bow down before him."

"Did they bring presents?" Whitby asked. "I like presents."

"Yes. They'd brought with them large treasure chests of gold, frankincense, and myrrh."

"I know what gold is, but what's frankincense?" asked Hector.

"Some kind of expensive perfume, I believe," Christopher Rabbit replied.

"And myrrh?"

"Isn't it used as an oil?" suggested Caravan Bear.

"Yes. I think oils and spices were rubbed onto people's bodies after they died," Christopher Rabbit explained.

"Why did they do that?" asked Whitby.

Christopher Rabbit shrugged. "It was what they did in those days."

"I expect it was also expensive," said Hector.

"So perhaps they were kings, not just wise men," Whitby thought out loud. "Otherwise they wouldn't have been able to afford expensive presents."

"Maybe," agreed Christopher Rabbit.

Whitby wrinkled her nose. "Funny sort of presents to give to a baby," she said. "Maybe he'd rather have had a toy to play with. Something like a rattle, or a ball."

Christopher Rabbit laughed. "When King Herod heard what the wise men said, he was very frightened."

"Why?" asked Whitby.

"If you were the king of the Jews and heard that another King of the Jews had been born, you might be a bit worried that the new king would want to get rid of you."

"I'm glad I'm not a king then," said Whitby. "I'm not very wise either."

"So what did he do?" asked Caravan Bear.

"King Herod called his officials and asked them where the baby was to be born. They told him that it had been written by a prophet that he would be born in a town called Bethlehem. Herod told the wise men to go there. He said that when they had found the baby, they should return to his palace and tell him how to get there so he could go and bow down before the new king."

"That was nice of him," said Whitby.

"Well, it wasn't actually, because – as we find later – Herod only wanted to find the baby to kill him."

"Not nice then."

"No."

"Didn't they have any maps?" asked Hector.

Christopher Rabbit shook his head. "I don't suppose so, because once they'd left King Herod, the wise men set out across the desert to look for Bethlehem. All they had to guide them was the special star, which moved ahead of them. When it stopped, they had reached Bethlehem."

"Just a minute," queried Hector. "Did they travel by night, then? Because they wouldn't have been able to see the star in the daytime."

"I suppose they must have done," Christopher Rabbit agreed. "Anyway, it would have been cooler to travel at night, as deserts are very hot during the day."

"Did they find the baby?" asked Whitby.

"Yes." Christopher Rabbit returned to his book. "The wise men went into the house…"

"I thought it was a stable…" said Whitby.

"… or barn," Hector muttered.

"It says 'house' in the Bible," said Christopher Rabbit firmly. "Perhaps by that time Mary, Joseph, and baby Jesus had moved to a house."

"Much more comfortable," remarked Caravan Bear.

"Oh, I don't know," said Hector. "I'd rather live in a stable than a house."

"Yes, but you're not God's son, are you?" asked Whitby.

Hector wrinkled his nose. "Not as far as I know," he said finally.

"The wise men opened their treasure chests and offered Jesus their presents of gold, frankincense, and myrrh," Christopher Rabbit went on.

"I remember being given a squeaky toy bone when I was a puppy," Whitby remarked. "It was a lovely present and I played with it a lot. I was very upset when I broke it," she finished sadly.

"Did they go back to King Herod after they'd seen the baby?" asked Caravan Bear. "I don't trust that king."

"No, they didn't. They had a dream warning them not to return to Jerusalem, so when they left Bethlehem, they took a different route home to their own country."

Everyone was silent for a while, listening to the night-time rustlings and murmurings as animals and birds found places to sleep. A couple of moths flitted in front of the light.

Who Jesus Was

"What did King Herod do?" asked Hector.

"He was furious at how he'd been tricked by the wise men," Christopher Rabbit went on. "He ordered his soldiers to go to Bethlehem and kill all the children up to the age of two."

"That's wicked!" cried Whitby.

"Why wasn't Jesus killed?" asked Caravan Bear.

"Joseph dreamed that one of God's angels came and told him to pack and leave straight away with Jesus and his mother, and take them to Egypt. And that's what they did. They didn't return until King Herod had died."

"Is that the end of the story?" asked Whitby.

"Well yes, that's the end of that story, but the story of Jesus goes on."

"Will you tell us more about Jesus?" Hector asked.

"Yes, of course, but not right now," Christopher Rabbit replied, closing the Bible.

"Time we were in bed," said Caravan Bear. He blew out the lamp and he and Whitby went into the caravan. Hector wandered away.

Christopher Rabbit stayed where he was. He leaned back and looked up at the inky black sky, which was filled with thousands of pinpoints of twinkling stars.

"I wonder how the wise men knew which star to follow?" he thought. The sky was very big and Christopher Rabbit felt very small. "God probably told them," he decided. "Thank you, God, for the story of the wise men who followed the special star to find baby Jesus. Help us to find Jesus as we go on our travels."

He sat for some time, staring up at the sky, then picked up his Bible, went into the warmth of the brightly lit caravan, and closed the door.

2

Jesus in the Temple

Christopher Rabbit held the reins gently.

"If you want Hector to turn left, you pull on the left-hand rein," Caravan Bear instructed. "And if you want him to turn right, you pull on the right-hand rein. And if you want Hector to stop, you pull on both reins."

Hector grinned as he towed the caravan along the road. "Or you could say 'stop', or 'halt', or 'whoa', and I might or might not do what you want depending on how I feel," he said, trotting faster.

The caravan bounced up and down and Christopher Rabbit had a job holding on.

"Slow down!" Caravan Bear shouted. "You're not being fair to Christopher Rabbit!"

Hector slowed. "Sorry," he said. "You just tell me what you want me to do, Christopher Rabbit, and

I'll do it – probably."

"It's all yours, Christopher Rabbit," Caravan Bear said, closing his eyes. "Any problems, just prod me awake."

Hector plodded on. Christopher Rabbit watched the road ahead. He felt it a great privilege to be trusted with the reins. He saw a pothole in the road and lightly pulled on the right-hand rein to stop Hector from stumbling into it.

"I did see it," Hector said. "But thank you for warning me."

Christopher Rabbit glowed with pride.

Sometime later, Caravan Bear woke with a jerk.

"I think we're almost there," he said, rubbing his eyes and looking around. "That's it. Pull off the road onto that patch of grass, Christopher Rabbit."

The caravan was soon parked in a small glade beside a stream.

"Not bad for a beginner," Hector said approvingly as Christopher Rabbit removed the harness from Hector's back.

"Thank you," replied Christopher Rabbit, heaving a big sigh of relief.

The caravan was soon made safe to stop it rolling down the slope into the stream.

"Do you remember that time when the caravan nearly ended up in a river?" Hector asked.

"Because I hadn't put bricks under its wheels," Caravan Bear added.

Christopher Rabbit nodded. "It was after I'd told you the story about the wise and foolish builders,

JESUS IN THE TEMPLE

wasn't it? Whitby, you remember it, don't you?"** He looked around. "Whitby?"

"Whitby!" called Caravan Bear. He went inside the caravan. "Whitby?" He came out, shaking his head. "She's not here."

The three of them walked around, calling out, "Whitby! Whitby!"

There was no reply.

"She's playing a game with us," said Hector uncertainly.

"I haven't seen her since before we moved on." Christopher Rabbit frowned. "But I was learning how to handle the reins and didn't think to see if she was with us."

"And I was busy teaching you," said Caravan Bear unhappily, "and didn't think about her."

He sat down heavily on the caravan steps.

"Oh dear, oh dear!"

Hector and Christopher Rabbit looked at each other.

"She can't have gone far," Christopher Rabbit said gently.

Caravan Bear sniffed. "I think we must have left her behind." He covered his face with his paws. "I can't bear the thought of losing her. She'll be so frightened."

"We'll go back," said Hector firmly.

"Don't worry," said Christopher Rabbit, "we'll find her."

Caravan Bear lifted his head. Tears were rolling down his cheeks and Christopher Rabbit was quite shocked. Caravan Bear had always seemed such a calm bear, quietly in charge of them all.

"We'll find her," he said again.

"I know she likes to run around and sometimes plays tricks on me but she's such a lovely, faithful little dog. Her mother gave her to me when she was a tiny puppy and she's been with me ever since." Caravan Bear wiped away his tears.

"Look, why don't you stay here, and Hector and I will go back and search for her," suggested Christopher Rabbit. "It'll save a lot of time if we don't have to hitch up the caravan and take it with us."

"Whatever you like," said Caravan Bear miserably.

"Fancy a ride?" Hector asked Christopher Rabbit, who looked up at the broad back of the horse and gulped. He had never ridden a horse before.

"Hop up," Hector said briskly. "You'll be quite safe."

So Christopher Rabbit hopped up and a moment later they were off. Hector galloped back down the road,

Jesus in the Temple

shouting "Whitby! Whitby!" while Christopher Rabbit closed his eyes and held tightly onto Hector's mane.

"You'll never see her if you keep your eyes closed!" Hector shouted.

Christopher Rabbit wondered how Hector knew his eyes were closed, and opened them in astonishment. The sides of the road flashed past them. He felt a bit

sick and hoped he wouldn't fall off.

"Whitby. Whitby," he called out timidly and began to feel better. He called louder and tried to see if he could spot a small brown dog, but there was no sign of her.

When they reached the place where they had last pitched their caravan, Christopher Rabbit slid off Hector's back and they looked at each other.

"You go that way, and I'll go this way," he said to Hector. "We'll meet back here in a few minutes."

Hector set off across the moor, calling out Whitby's name.

Christopher Rabbit closed his eyes for a moment.

"Please, God, help us find Whitby," he said. Then he went off in the other direction.

He reached the edge of the moor and plunged into a thicket of bushes.

"Whitby! Whitby!"

"Looking for someone?" asked a blackbird perched on the branch of a bush.

"You haven't seen a small dog, have you? Her name's Whitby and we've lost her."

The blackbird shook her head from side to side. "Haven't seen any small dog," she said. "But I saw two large dogs some time ago. They come from around here."

"Do you know where they live?" Christopher Rabbit asked. "Whitby might have gone with them. She likes making new friends."

The blackbird jerked her head. "I think they're from that farmhouse over there. Tell you what, I'll fly that way and if I see her I'll tell her you're looking for her."

"Oh, would you? Thank you so much," Christopher Rabbit replied gratefully.

He retraced his steps and soon came across Hector, who shook his head.

"No sign."

"We'll go to that farmhouse, Hector. A blackbird told me Whitby might have gone off with two dogs who live there."

"Just wait until I see her," Hector growled, trotting briskly in the direction of the farmhouse. "She'll get a good talking-to from me for frightening us all and upsetting Caravan Bear."

"I just hope she's all right," panted Christopher Rabbit, running alongside.

They found Whitby just outside the farm. The blackbird, who was sitting on a stone wall, flew to meet them.

"I told her you were looking for her," the blackbird told them.

"Thank you so much for your help," said Christopher Rabbit.

"Pleasure, I'm sure," twitted the bird and flew off.

Christopher Rabbit, Hector, and Whitby looked at each other.

"What's the matter?" asked Whitby.

"Matter?" exploded Hector. "Matter? We've been searching everywhere for you! I've never seen Caravan Bear so upset!"

"But I thought we weren't moving on for ages," Whitby stammered. "I met these two very nice dogs and we got talking and they asked me if I'd like to look at their home, so I said I would."

"And you never thought to tell Caravan Bear?" asked Hector angrily.

"Well, no."

"Never mind," said Christopher Rabbit. "We ought to be getting back. Caravan Bear will be so worried."

He and Whitby climbed onto Hector's back, and they set off at a gallop back to where the caravan was parked.

Caravan Bear was overjoyed when they all arrived.

Jesus in the Temple

"I'm really sorry I upset you," Whitby said in a small voice.

"Never mind," smiled Caravan Bear. "You're back home with us now."

They had something to eat and sat around the fire. They were all tired but somehow didn't want to go to bed just yet.

"Can you tell us another story about Jesus?" Caravan Bear asked suddenly. "If you're not too tired, that is. I want to know what happened after he and his family came back from Egypt."

Christopher Rabbit took his Bible down from the shelf where he kept it. He opened it and began to laugh.

"What's so funny?" asked Hector, munching the grass right beside the caravan door.

"You'll see in a minute," Christopher Rabbit replied.

"When Mary, Joseph, and Jesus returned from Egypt, they settled in a town called Nazareth. When Jesus was twelve years old, the family went to Jerusalem to a big festival."

"What were they doing in Nazareth?" asked Caravan Bear.

Christopher Rabbit looked at the Bible.

"I don't know – it doesn't say. The Bible does say that Joseph was a carpenter, so he probably went back to the same job. He might have opened a shop."

Christopher Rabbit went back to the story. "The festival the family went to in Jerusalem was called Passover. It was held to celebrate God rescuing his people from Egypt."

"Why was it called Passover?" asked Whitby.

"Do you remember the story about God sending different horrible plagues to the people of Egypt in order to persuade the pharaoh to free the Israelite slaves?*

"The last plague was that every firstborn child would die, but the angel of death would pass over the houses of the Israelites and those children wouldn't die."

"So that's why it's called 'Passover' – the angel of death passed over the slaves' houses," said Hector thoughtfully. "I like that."

"Every year from then it was celebrated in a great week-long festival. People would travel for miles from all over the country to come to Jerusalem. It was all very exciting for Mary, Joseph,

and Jesus, and I expect they had a wonderful time," Christopher Rabbit said.

"Was that the first time Jesus had gone to the festival?" asked Hector.

"Quite possibly. After it was over, people started leaving the city to return to their homes. Mary and Joseph left along with a whole crowd of relatives and friends. They journeyed all day and it wasn't until they stopped for the night that they realized that Jesus wasn't with them."

"A bit like us and Whitby," murmured Hector.

"When did you realize I wasn't with you?" asked Whitby.

"Not until we reached this spot," Caravan Bear replied. "We thought you were either in the caravan or running around."

"I was learning how to manage the reins and I'm afraid I didn't think about you at all," Christopher Rabbit admitted honestly.

"And I was helping Christopher Rabbit," Hector said smugly.

"And I'm afraid I went to sleep," said Caravan Bear.

"Huh! Fine friends!" Whitby muttered.

"We should have realized earlier that you weren't with us," admitted Christopher Rabbit, "but we did go back for you straight away. And Mary and Joseph went straight back to Jerusalem once they realized that Jesus wasn't with them. When they reached the city they searched everywhere, asking everyone they met whether they'd seen a twelve-year-old boy. They probably described him, too."

Jesus in the Temple

"I wonder if they asked the birds to help?" Hector pondered. "The blackbird was very helpful when we were looking for you, Whitby."

"They searched for three days without finding Jesus," Christopher Rabbit went on. "Finally, they went into the large courtyards surrounding the Temple."

"What was the Temple?" asked Whitby.

"The Temple was, I think, the holiest place in the country. Only priests could go into the actual building, but around it were huge courtyards. In them, Jewish teachers would discuss and study holy writings, which were called Scripture. People met there to offer sacrifices to God and celebrate at festivals. They were always very busy places, crowded with people.

"Mary and Joseph walked around these enormous courtyards, searching for Jesus. At last someone pointed him out. He was sitting in the middle of a group of much older men, listening to what was being said and asking questions. Mary and Joseph ran over to him. 'How could you behave like this?' his mother asked. 'We've been so worried about you. We've searched everywhere.'"

"Rather like Christopher Rabbit and I did," said Hector.

"The teachers told Mary and Joseph that Jesus' questions and comments had amazed them. The boy, they said, had a very good understanding of the Scriptures. Well, he might have been clever, but that didn't stop Mary and Joseph from telling Jesus off for having frightened them. Jesus looked up at them, surprised. 'Why have you been searching for me?' he asked. 'Didn't you realize that I would be in my Father's house?'"

"That was a funny thing to say," said Hector.

"What did he mean by it?" asked Caravan Bear. "Wasn't his home in Nazareth with Mary and Joseph?"

Christopher Rabbit thought for a minute. "I think he must have been talking about the Temple, which was sometimes called the house of God. Jesus called God 'Father'."

"Do you think he knew he was God's son?" asked Hector.

"He might have done."

"Did Mary and Joseph know what Jesus meant?"

Christopher Rabbit shook his head. "No. They didn't understand him at all. They were just glad to have found him. They took him home to Nazareth and Jesus never did anything like that again. But he

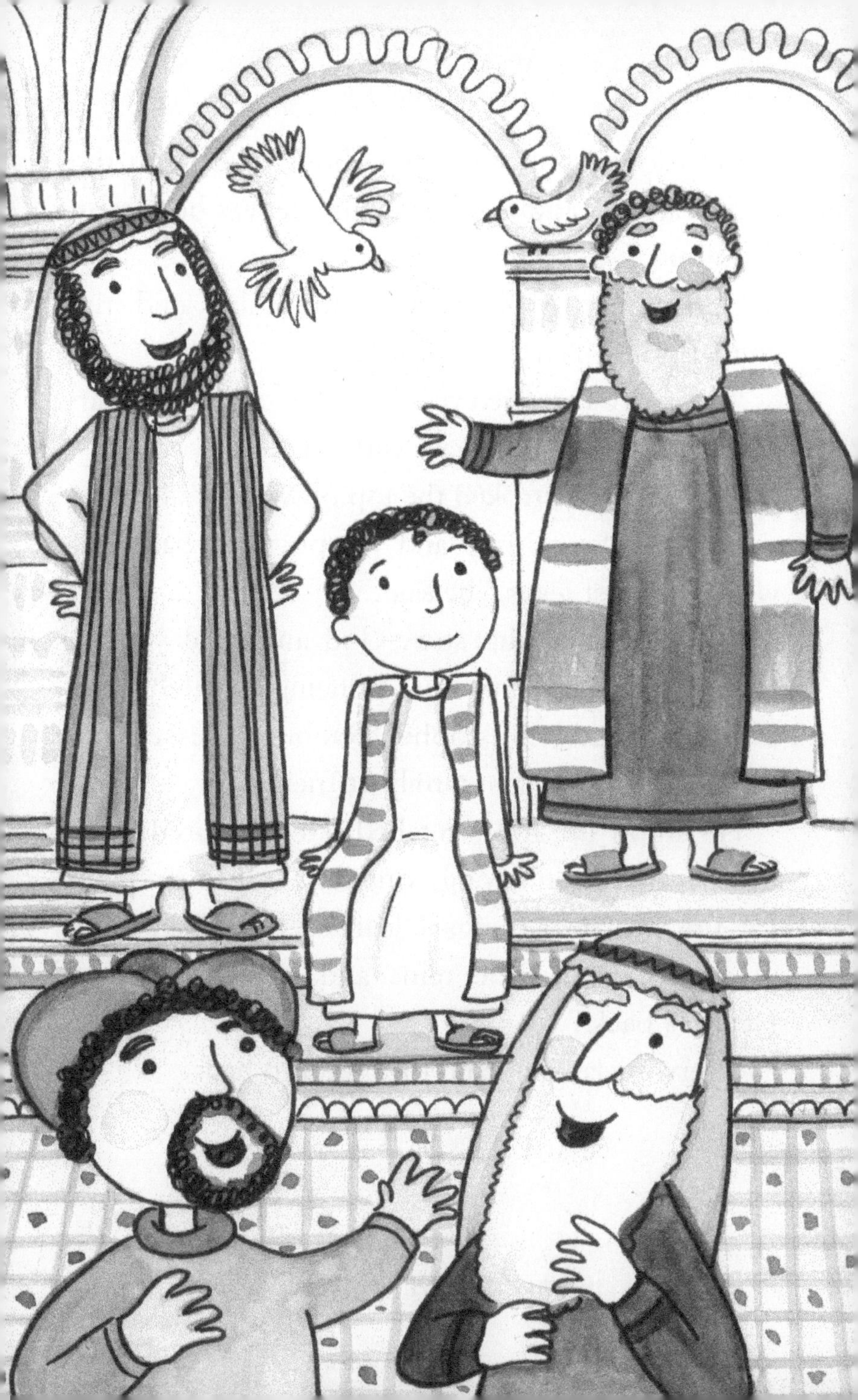

spent a lot of time learning about God from the local teachers, and as he grew up, he was both wise and good."

Christopher Rabbit closed the Bible and the animals were silent for a moment.

"I'm sorry I worried you," Whitby said to Caravan Bear. "I won't go off again without telling you."

Caravan Bear stroked the top of Whitby's head.

"I know how Mary and Joseph must have felt when they lost Jesus," he said.

"Thank you for that story, God, and thank you for helping us find Whitby and bringing us safely back together," said Christopher Rabbit. "Please help everyone who has lost family or friends."

He stood up and stretched. He was tired, very tired. It had been a long, long day. "And thank you for the two new things I learned today," he said. "How to handle the reins and how to stay on Hector's back."

Everyone laughed and they went to bed.

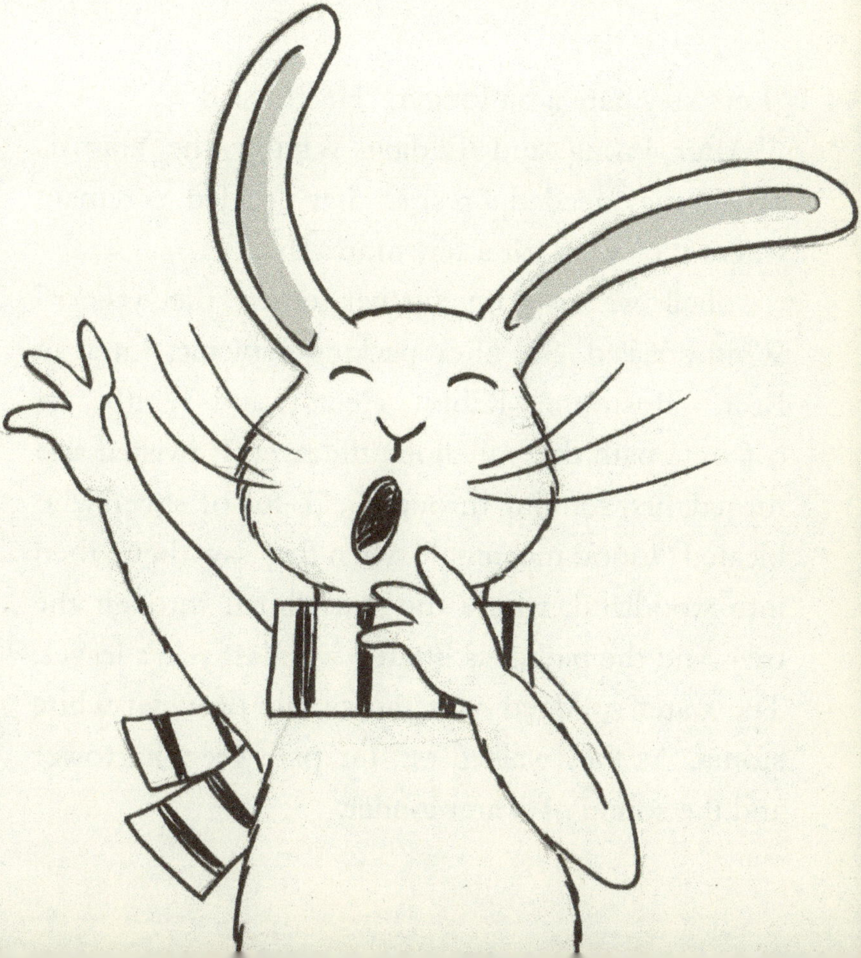

Jesus is Baptized

"Let's stay here a bit longer," Hector said.

After losing and finding Whitby, the animals agreed they needed a rest so they decided to remain where they were for a few more days.

"Shall we explore further down the valley?" Whitby asked. So, after packing a picnic, Caravan Bear, Christopher Rabbit, Hector, and Whitby set off on a path that ran along the river. It twisted and turned, first running through fields full of sheep who bleated "Good morning!" when they saw them, then into woodland, where the sun glinted through the trees and the path was littered with last year's leaves. The water sparkled as it ran swiftly over flat white stones. As they walked on, the path grew narrower and the sound of water louder.

Jesus is Baptized

"Shall we stop for something to eat?" asked Whitby hopefully.

Caravan Bear looked ahead. "There might be somewhere to sit a bit further on."

The path suddenly turned sharply to the left. The animals stopped. Ahead of them, the river ran into a pool of clear water, fed by a shimmering waterfall, which flashed and sparkled in the sun.

"Oh!" breathed Christopher Rabbit. "That's so beautiful."

"I'm going in," cried Whitby and she ran into the pool. "It's so cold, but it's *so* good!" she shouted. "Come and join me!"

Hector, Christopher Rabbit, and Caravan Bear plunged into the pool after her. It was wonderful! They dived through the waterfall, they splashed each other, they shouted and laughed.

When they were thoroughly wet and very hungry, they returned to the bank and ate their picnic.

"I'm so glad we stayed," said Whitby, grabbing a sandwich.

After eating every crumb of food they had, they started back along the path. The sound of the waterfall faded, and another sound took over: the sound of sheep. They rounded the corner and found their way blocked.

"Hello," said the sheep nearest to them. "We thought we'd follow you and see where you were going. It gets very boring wandering around the field all day."

"We've had a swim in the pool and a picnic, and now we're going back to the caravan," said Caravan Bear.

"So would you mind letting us through?" Hector asked.

With much jostling and pushing, the sheep moved off the path, and Christopher Rabbit, Hector, Caravan

Bear, and Whitby squeezed past. As they went, they noticed that each sheep had a dab of a different colour on its fleece.

"What are those marks for?" asked Whitby.

"They let the shepherds know who we belong to," said one of the sheep, pushing another almost into the river.

At last the path was clear and the friends made their way back to their caravan.

"What an adventure!" said Whitby.

"Would you like to finish off the day with a story?" asked Christopher Rabbit. The animals agreed and Christopher Rabbit fetched his Bible.

"Jesus had a relative whose name was John," he said, beginning to read. "He was a little bit older than Jesus and when he had grown up, he left his home and went to live a rough life out in the desert. He wore a camel-skin coat tied around the waist with a leather belt. It was a very hard life. The desert was hot and there was little to eat except wild honey and locusts."

"Ugh," Whitby pulled a face. "Why did he do that?"

"That was the only food he could find."

"I mean, why did he live in the desert?"

"He wanted to find out what God wanted him to do. God told him to preach, and soon crowds of people were flocking from nearby towns and villages to hear what he had to say. John wasn't afraid to talk about what he believed. He told people that God's kingdom was coming and that they needed to be sorry for the bad things they had done and begin to live the kind of lives God wanted for them.

Jesus is Baptized

"They thought that John might be the one that the people were waiting for – the messiah, the promised king. John told them that he wasn't the one. He said that it would be someone coming after him. What he said made sense to many of the people who came to hear him. They were really sorry for breaking God's laws and wanted to start new lives. So John baptized them in the River Jordan, inviting them down into the river with him, and dipping them under the water."

"Bit of a funny thing to do if you ask me," Hector murmured.

Christopher Rabbit thought for a moment. "Do you remember how we felt after we'd swum in the pool?"

"Clean," said Whitby.

"Refreshed," said Caravan Bear.

"Yes, clean and refreshed," agreed Christopher Rabbit. "I think being baptized is a sign that God has forgiven us and that he has given us a clean, fresh start."

The animals thought about this.

"So where does Jesus come into it?" asked Hector.

"Well, when John, who became known as John the Baptist, was baptizing people in the River

Jordan, Jesus came along and asked John to baptize him, too."

"Why did he do that?" asked Caravan Bear. "I mean, Jesus was God's son, wasn't he? He'd never done anything bad in his life so he didn't need to be forgiven by God."

"John thought the same," Christopher Rabbit replied. "He couldn't see why Jesus wanted to be baptized. Jesus was, John said, a much better person than he was. He told the crowds that he wasn't fit to untie the laces on Jesus' sandals. But Jesus told John that this was what God wanted. He wanted John to baptize him."

"Why?" asked Whitby.

Christopher Rabbit shook his head. "I don't know."

"Do you think," Hector began, "it might be because although Jesus was God's Son, he was also human, and that's what humans needed to do?"

"Perhaps he wanted to be baptized as an example to others?" Caravan Bear wondered.

"Was Jesus grown up by then?" Whitby asked suddenly.

"Yes, he was," Christopher Rabbit said.

"Well, perhaps he had done bad things, things he was ashamed of, and he wanted to be made clean and right with God," suggested Whitby.

Jesus is Baptized

Christopher Rabbit shook his head. "I don't think that's what it was. I think, more likely, he was just doing what God wanted. Whatever the reason, Jesus insisted that John baptize him," Christopher Rabbit went on. "So John did. And when Jesus came up out of the water, a strange thing happened. It seemed as if the clouds of heaven opened and a dove came down and rested on Jesus. A voice said, "You are my Son, whom I love, and I am pleased with you."

"Gosh," said Whitby. "Was that God?"

"Yes."

"I'm not sure I'd like it if God spoke to me like that."

"Oh, I don't know," said Hector. "I think that if God said to me, 'You are my horse, whom I love, and I am pleased with you,' it would be quite nice."

"God wants to tell us all that he loves us," Christopher Rabbit said thoughtfully.

"Yes, but he doesn't send a dove down to sit on my head and speak from the clouds," Hector argued.

"Anyway, he might love Hector, but he might not be pleased with him," remarked Whitby. "And I shouldn't think he's pleased with me, as I do naughty things all the time."

"But you are sorry when you do them," said Caravan Bear.

"Not at the time. I'm only sorry afterwards."

"God didn't say, 'You are Jesus, whom I love, and I am pleased with you,'" explained Christopher Rabbit. "He said, 'You are my Son,' which is different. He wouldn't call you his son, Hector."

The animals had been concentrating on the story, and it was only when Christopher Rabbit stopped

Jesus is Baptized

speaking that they became aware of a sound around them. They looked out through the open door of the caravan and saw sheep. A lot of sheep, crowding around the door and looking in through the windows.

"We wanted to see the caravan so we followed you," said one of the sheep.

"Then we started listening to the story and didn't want to disturb you," added another. "We'll go now."

Christopher Rabbit left the caravan. It seemed rude to stay inside when the sheep were outside. Caravan Bear and Whitby followed him.

"I hope you liked the story," Christopher Rabbit said as he jumped down the steps.

"Oh yes. Very interesting." The first sheep turned, then stopped. "Oh dear, I've forgotten the way back to my field."

"So have I," said another, and all the sheep began bleating.

Caravan Bear raised a paw. "Just a minute," he said. "I've had an idea."

The sheep quietened down.

"You told Whitby that the coloured marks let the shepherds know who you belong to, didn't you?"

The sheep nodded.

"Well in that case, if you sort yourselves out into groups of colours, it'll be easier for the shepherds to take you back to the sheepfolds you belong in."

It took some time but at last all the sheep were separated into their groups. Green ones, red ones, and black ones.

"Now what?" asked the first sheep, who seemed to speak for them all.

Jesus is Baptized

Just then, three vehicles arrived and screeched to a halt. Out sprung three shepherds.

"Come along, green sheep. Follow me." He looked at Caravan Bear. "Thank you for sorting them. Saved us a lot of trouble."

Soon the different groups of sheep were led off by the shepherds. The friends looked at each other.

"That was clever of you, Caravan Bear," Hector said admiringly.

"Aren't sheep silly?" remarked Whitby.

"Perhaps being baptized is like the mark on a sheep. It's a sign that you belong to Jesus," Caravan Bear said thoughtfully.

"Perhaps," agreed Christopher Rabbit.

"Unlike the sheep," murmured Whitby, "who don't know who they belong to."

"Thank you, God, for a lovely day," said Hector.

"And thank you for the story," added Caravan Bear.

"And thank you especially for Jesus, who you sent to show us that we belong to you. Help us to follow you," said Christopher Rabbit.

4

In the Wilderness

"Funny place, this," muttered Hector, puffing hard as he towed the caravan up hills and down hills.

"You think everywhere is funny," Whitby retorted, running beside him.

"It's all right for you – you haven't got to pull this heavy caravan," Hector grumbled.

"Funny old Hector, always grumbling," Whitby laughed and ran off up the road.

"It's not a funny place, it's just different from anywhere we've ever been before," Caravan Bear said from his seat on the caravan's steps.

Christopher Rabbit looked from side to side with interest. It was a hot day and the sun beat down from a clear blue sky. There were few trees, and those he saw were small, stunted ones clinging to the peaty earth and springy heather. There were no fields. Round, grey rocks, some big, some small, littered the landscape as far as the eye could see. Here and there were clumps of sweet-smelling bright yellow gorse in full flower.

"It looks lovely now, but it probably looks very different on dull days," he thought.

The road grew increasingly narrow, running through high banks of bare rock. There was only just enough room for the caravan to pass.

"I hope I don't meet any other caravans," Hector muttered.

There was the toot of a horn and a large car swept around the corner toward them.

Hector pulled up sharply and closed his eyes. There was a squeal of brakes and the approaching car just managed to stop in time.

A woman leaned out of the window and shouted, "You'll have to go back down the road!"

"He can't," said Caravan Bear, jumping off the steps. "It isn't wide enough to turn around."

"Can't you reverse your car back up the road?" Christopher Rabbit asked the driver.

The woman sighed. "I suppose I'll have to. Didn't you see the passing place?"

"What passing place?"

The woman sighed again. "On narrow roads like this, there are places where two vehicles can pass each other. You need to look out for them."

"Sorry," said Caravan Bear.

"Sorry," said Hector.

The woman began backing her car slowly up the road. When she reached the passing place, she pulled in and waited for Hector and the caravan to pass.

"There are falling rocks a bit further on!" she called as the caravan went by. "Better watch out!"

"Thank you," Caravan Bear shouted back, and they drove on.

"I suppose you know what you're doing, Caravan Bear, but I don't think I like this place one little bit," said Hector.

"I like it," said Whitby. She looked up at Hector. "You're just a misery. You wanted adventure, and this is it."

Hector sniffed. "All I ever wanted was a quiet life."

Bang! Thud!

Small rocks and stones were rolling down the banks onto the road, and Hector picked up speed. The caravan raced along, swaying from side to side.

Stones bounced off the roof and Caravan Bear winced. "Ouch! My poor caravan!"

"We need hard hats!" Whitby shouted, jumping up onto the steps and crouching beside Caravan Bear.

Thud! Bang!

The steep banks came to an end and, with a final bang on the caravan's roof from one last stone, the road became wider, much to everyone's relief.

Hector slowed down.

"Are you all right, Hector?" Christopher Rabbit asked.

"Well, I wasn't hit," Hector replied sourly and plodded on.

The sun was hanging low in the sky when he finally came to a stop on a grassy bank beside the road.

"That's it," he said. "I've had enough."

He lowered his head and began to graze.

Whitby jumped down, her tail wagging furiously.

"Just look!"

Christopher Rabbit and Caravan Bear climbed down from the caravan.

They were parked on the edge of a bank that led steeply down to a brilliant blue sea. Far below them white waves lapped gently around the shores of hundreds of small islands.

"That's so beautiful," Christopher Rabbit said quietly.

"It's like looking down on the world," Whitby declared.

Far in the distance, the sun, a great golden ball, dipped below the horizon.

"Did you know it would be like this?" Hector asked.

"I saw a picture and thought it would be fun to come," Caravan Bear replied. "I didn't know about the rocks, though," he added worriedly. "I'd better see what damage they've done to the roof."

They unhitched Hector and set up the caravan.

"I'm hungry," said Whitby.

"You're always hungry," Hector grinned.

Caravan Bear climbed onto the roof and started inspecting the damage.

"It'll take quite a bit of work to mend," he said, shaking his head.

"It doesn't need to be mended now, does it?" asked Whitby anxiously. "We don't have to go home, do we?"

Caravan Bear climbed down.

"No, we don't have to go home."

"Have we got to go back the way we came?" Christopher Rabbit asked.

"Probably," Caravan Bear said gloomily. "That'll mean more rocks."

"I'm hungry," Whitby said again, more loudly.

"Right. Supper," said Caravan Bear. "Just as well we've brought food with us! I don't think there's a shop for miles."

"If we get stuck here, Whitby, you'll starve," said Hector teasingly. "I won't starve because I can graze anywhere."

"I do wish you two would stop bickering," Caravan Bear said, sticking his head out of the door.

"He started it," said Whitby.

"I didn't, you did," said Hector.

"Anyway, it's not bickering," Whitby added.

Hector moved away. It wasn't fair, he thought. He did the work of pulling the heavy caravan and all Whitby did was make fun of him and tell him he was old. He wasn't old. He sighed, thinking back to the time when he was a young, proud horse. His coat had been brushed until it shone, and he had worn a harness and saddle studded with bright stones. Ribbons had been plaited into his tail.

He hummed a tune to himself, then sighed again. That was all a long, long time ago, before he had been sold to the farmer who had beaten him. And then Caravan Bear had bought him and been good to him. He didn't mind going off on adventures — but a warm stable, a thick coat in winter, plenty of oats, and the odd carrot and apple would make him very happy. Perhaps, he thought, he *was* getting old.

After supper, they sat for a long time until it was quite dark. Whitby shivered suddenly.

"It's a bit eerie," she said.

It was true. The darkness seemed to press down on them.

"I think this must be the wildest place we've ever come to," said Christopher Rabbit.

"It's a real adventure," said Whitby uncertainly, keeping close to Caravan Bear as they went into the caravan. "It is, isn't it?"

Caravan Bear lit the lamps and closed the door.

Hector put his head in through the window.

"Can we have a story?" he asked.

"Are you sure you want one?" Christopher Rabbit replied, thinking that it was quite late, and he was quite tired.

"Yes, of course," said Caravan Bear. "It might take my mind off the damaged caravan."

Christopher Rabbit fetched his Bible and opened it.

"After Jesus had been baptized, he went into the desert," he began. "It was a wild place with nothing but sand and rocks for miles and miles. There wasn't any food and Jesus didn't eat for forty days."

"I'd have starved to death," Whitby said.

"Well, Jesus didn't, but I can imagine he was pretty hungry," Christopher Rabbit agreed.

"And thirsty, too," Whitby added.

"Why did he go into the desert?" Hector asked.

"I imagine he wanted to get away from everyone, to try and think about what God was asking him to do," said Christopher Rabbit. "From the moment he had been baptized, he knew that God had chosen him for some special work – something only he could do. I think he wanted to pray about it."

"Is praying harder when there are other people around?" asked Caravan Bear.

In the Wilderness

"It can be," said Christopher Rabbit after some thought. "Other people and other things can get in the way."

"Like thinking about the damage to the caravan roof?" Hector suggested slyly, looking at Caravan Bear.

"Right," said Whitby. "So there was Jesus, starving in the desert, which we all would be if Caravan Bear hadn't brought enough food."

"Except we're not in a desert," Hector reminded her.

"It might not be a desert, but it's pretty wild outside. What happened then?"

"Jesus was tempted by the devil," Christopher Rabbit went on.

"By the who?" asked Hector.

"Oh, Hector!" Whitby snapped impatiently.

"According to a very old story, the devil was an angel who was thrown out of heaven because he thought he was as good as God," Christopher Rabbit said. "Even worse: He wanted to be God and rule the universe."

"I didn't know angels were like that," Whitby remarked. "All the ones you've told us about in other stories were good. They were God's messengers."

"Well, *this* angel wasn't good. He was the source of everything bad and he was determined to stop Jesus from obeying God."

"Why was it so important for the devil to stop Jesus?" Hector asked.

"Jesus had just been baptized," Christopher Rabbit said, thoughtfully. "God had called him his Son and said he was pleased with him. I think Jesus must have realized then that God had given him a really important job to do – to show people what God was really like and bring them close to him. The devil wanted to stop that. So when Jesus was starving, the devil said to him, 'Why go hungry? If you're the Son of God, why don't you order these stones to turn into bread?'"

"That sounded like a good idea," Whitby said. "And did he?"

"No. Jesus said it's written in the Bible that humans can't live on bread alone."

"I live on oats and hay," Hector chipped in, "and the occasional carrot and apple if I'm lucky." He looked wistfully at Caravan Bear, who laughed and gave him an apple.

"If you're the Son of God, you can do what you want, can't you?" Whitby objected. "So why would it have been wrong to turn the stones into bread?"

"Wouldn't that have been setting himself up against God?" asked Caravan Bear slowly. "Doing what *he* wanted, not what *God* wanted?"

"I think so," Christopher Rabbit replied.

"Didn't some people set themselves up against God in one of the other stories you read us?" asked Hector, munching his apple. "You know, the ones who built a very high tower as they wanted to reach heaven and prove that they were more important than God?"*

"I think people have always done that," said Christopher Rabbit sadly. He read on. "Then the devil led Jesus to a high place. Jesus looked down and could see the whole world stretched out below him."

"A bit like the view of all the islands from the top of this bank," Whitby commented.

"The devil said that if Jesus were to worship him, instead of God, he would give Jesus the world to rule over," Christopher Rabbit continued.

"I don't think that would tempt me," said Caravan Bear. "Too much bother, looking after the whole world. It's hard enough looking after my caravan." He was still thinking about the damage to the roof.

"Oh, I don't know," said Whitby, her eyes shining. "If I owned all the world, I could have all the food I could eat and all the toys I wanted to play with."

"You'd just get fat," Hector said sarcastically.

"And Hector would have to stop being rude to me," Whitby finished.

"What did Jesus say?" asked Caravan Bear.

"He said that God is the only one we should worship and obey."

"What happened then?" asked Hector.

"The devil took Jesus to the highest point of the Temple in Jerusalem. 'If you really are the Son of God,' he said, 'throw yourself down from here. You needn't worry because God says in the Bible that he'll take care of you and stop you from hurting yourself.' Jesus replied by saying that it's wrong to test God's kindness to us."

"You mean," said Whitby, thinking about this, "that I shouldn't do something naughty like…"

"… like jumping on and off the roof of the caravan?" Caravan Bear finished. "I keep telling you that you might hurt yourself, and I can't always be there to catch you."

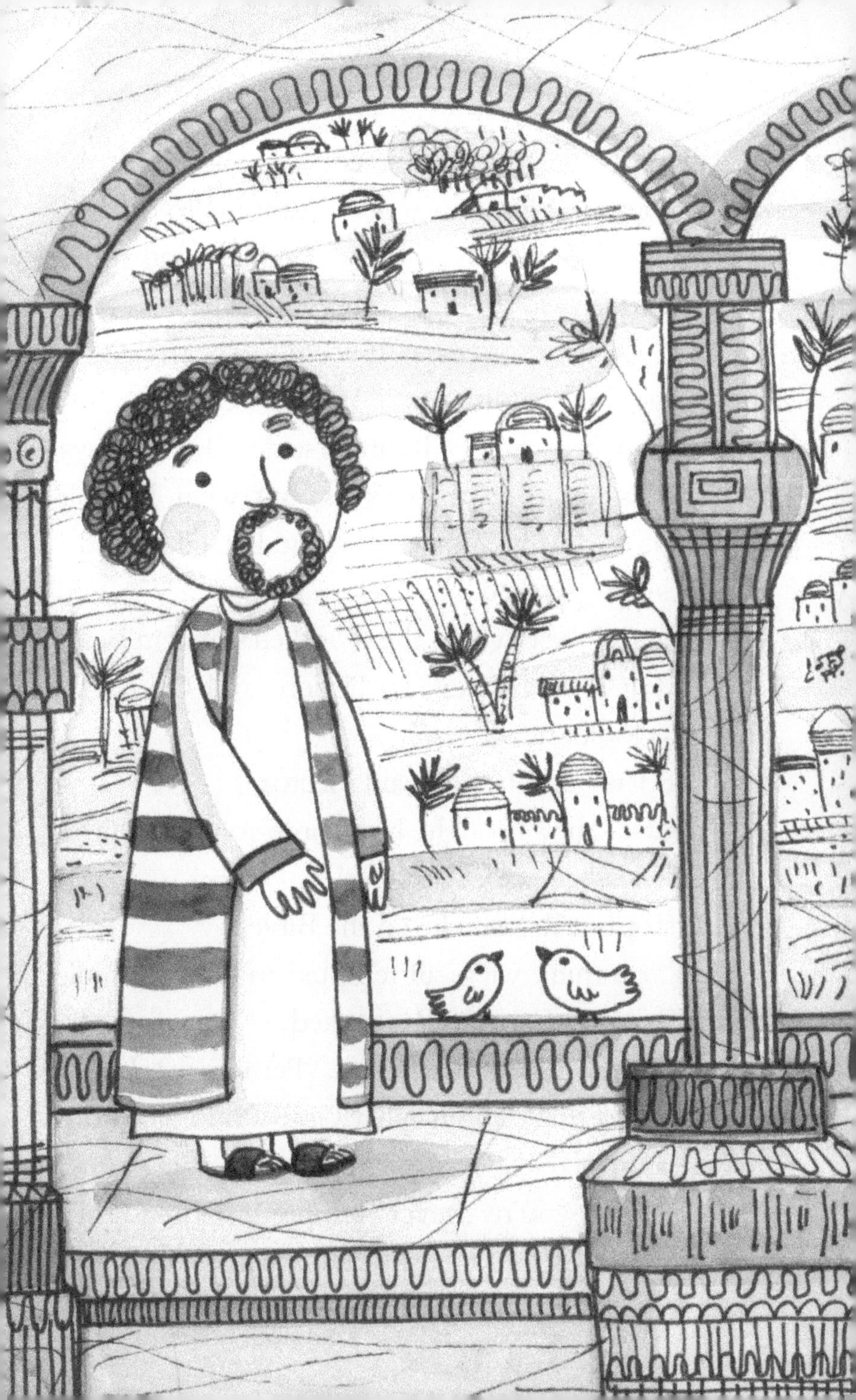

"All right," Whitby agreed. "I shouldn't do something that I know you don't want me to do. But if I do, I know you'll be there to catch me and you'll forgive me anyway. Is that what you mean?"

"God always forgives us if we're sorry for doing the wrong thing, doesn't he?" asked Hector.

"Yes," Christopher Rabbit said. "He always forgives us and always loves us, but what I think Jesus was saying was that we shouldn't take God's goodness for granted."

"What did the devil do then?" asked Caravan Bear.

"He knew he'd failed, so he left, and God sent angels to look after Jesus."

"Good angels I hope," said Hector.

"I expect they brought him some food," Whitby said practically.

Christopher Rabbit closed the Bible.

"Do you think we're all tempted to do and think wrong things?" Caravan Bear asked.

"Yes," said Christopher Rabbit. "Perhaps we should always try to think about what God wants us to do, and ask him to make us strong enough to obey him."

"I'm sure you're never tempted, Christopher Rabbit," Whitby said in a shocked voice.

"Oh, I am. We all are."

"I suppose I'm tempted too," Whitby said.

"To eat too much?" asked Hector.

"To be jealous of you," Whitby muttered.

"Jealous of Hector?" Caravan Bear asked, surprised. "Why?"

"I suppose…" Whitby began in a small voice. "I suppose because I've thought you might like him better than you like me. Before you rescued Hector, I was your dog and your special friend. And Hector's clever and strong and tows the caravan. I just get in everybody's way."

"That's silly," Caravan Bear replied strongly.

"I might be strong but I'm not clever," Hector said. "I'm really just a bad-tempered, stupid old horse."

"I should have realized you felt like that," Caravan Bear said to Whitby. He thought for a moment. "Perhaps, like Jesus, I've been tempted to think more about the caravan than about all of you."

"Jesus didn't have a caravan," said Whitby, brightening up.

"No, but he was tempted by the devil to think of what *he* wanted and not what *God* wanted."

"We're all tempted by different things," Christopher Rabbit said. "Perhaps we should ask God to help us follow Jesus' way and put *God* first, and not ourselves."

They said goodnight and went to bed.

Sometime later, Christopher Rabbit woke up. He looked out the window. There was a full moon, and by its silver light he could see Hector. The horse was humming and swaying gently from side to side.

"Do you think he's all right?" Caravan Bear asked quietly, joining Christopher Rabbit at the window.

They watched as Hector lifted a forefoot, pointed it, and pawed the ground. Then he did the same with the other one.

"What's going on?" whispered Whitby, who had woken and joined the other two.

"I think… I think he's dancing," Christopher Rabbit said quietly.

They watched for a little while longer. Hector turned his head from one side to the other, then bowed as if to an audience. Then he bent his head to the grass and quietly began to graze.

"I never knew," breathed Caravan Bear.

"What?" asked Whitby.

"I didn't know where Hector had been before we found him at the farm where he'd been badly treated."

"Do you think he was a circus horse?" Christopher Rabbit asked.

"Perhaps. I don't know." Caravan Bear fell silent.

"I don't think we should tell him we've seen him," Christopher Rabbit said, turning from the window.

"No. If he wants to tell us, he will," Caravan Bear said. "And perhaps God will help me think more about important things like my friends rather than my caravan," he added quietly.

"And I'll try not to tease Hector so much," said Whitby. "Although I'm not good at keeping promises."

Caravan Bear laughed. "I think he rather likes being teased," he said.

It was a long time before Christopher Rabbit went to sleep. He lay in his bed, cosy and warm, and thought about everything that had happened that day.

He smiled. "Thank you, God, for my friends," he said quietly. "Help us all to do our best to listen to you and obey you – because you love us and know what's best for us."

With that, he turned over and went back to sleep.

5

Jesus in Jerusalem

"I've had a thought about where we go next," said Caravan Bear.

"Where's that?" asked Whitby.

"You remember Miranda, the donkey we met?"

"The one we took to the donkey sanctuary?"***

"That's right. Well, I've had a message from her. She sent it by pigeon, but it's taken a long time to get here as the pigeon took ages to find us. Miranda said that she's settled in well and would love to see us if we're passing that way."

Hector shrugged. "I don't mind, if everyone's happy about it."

No one else did mind so they set off that morning. They were obviously expected and were made to feel very welcome when they arrived.

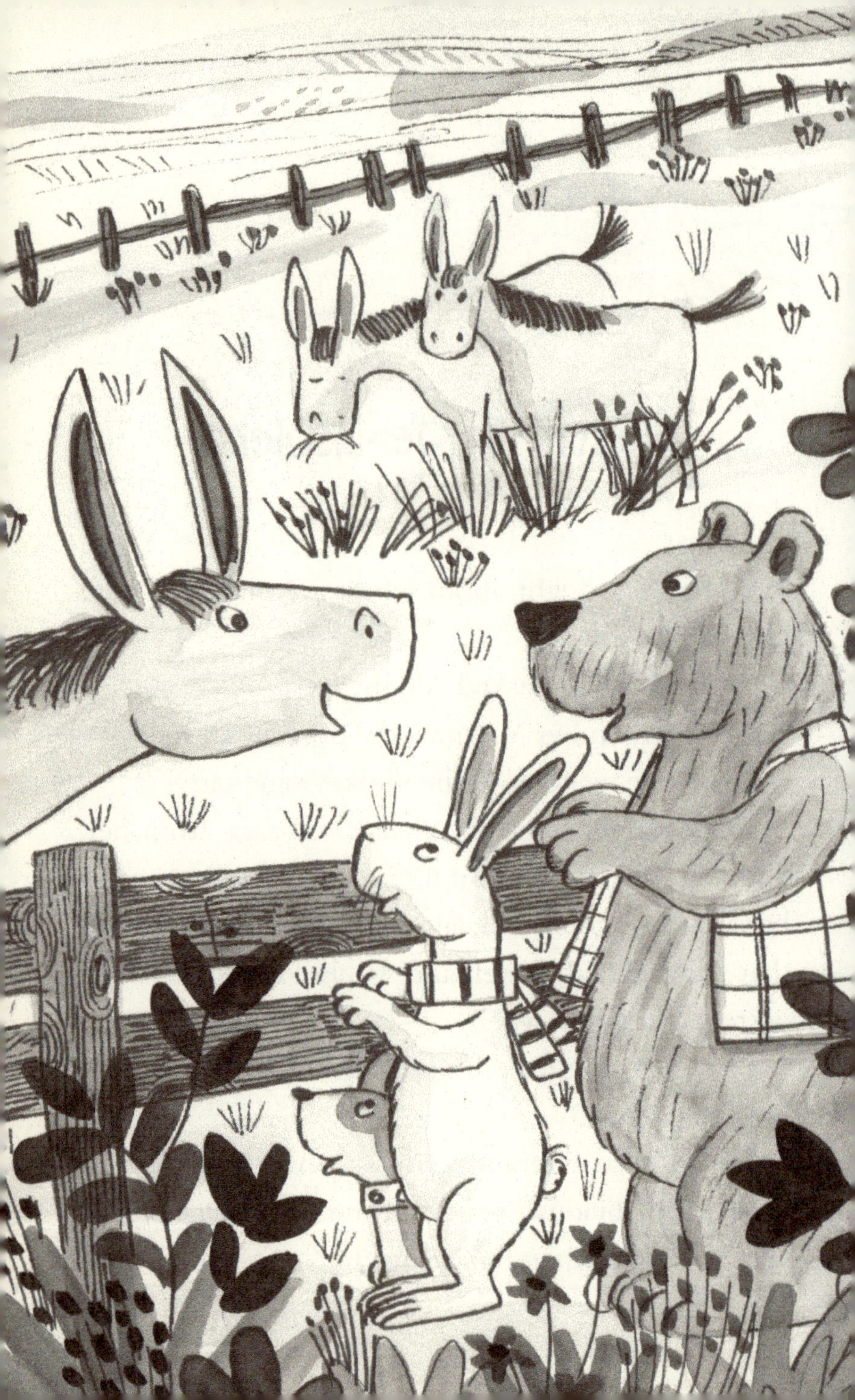

Hector looked around. "Lots of donkeys here. Makes me nervous."

"Why?" asked Christopher Rabbit.

"I feel outnumbered."

And there *were* lots of donkeys, grazing on the green square in the middle of the sanctuary, wandering around, talking in groups.

"How lovely to see you all!"

It was Miranda. She came trotting over.

"It's lovely to see you, too," said Caravan Bear. "You're looking really well."

Miranda's coat was brushed and she was glowing with health.

"It's all thanks to you. I love it here. And I've a surprise to show you. I'd like you to meet my daughter, Chloe."

A young donkey, who had trotted up behind her mother, moved forward.

"Do you like it here, too?" Hector asked her.

"S'all right," Chloe replied. "Gets a bit boring, though. Not much to do and most of the donkeys here are old."

"Most of the donkeys here have been rescued from people who treated them badly," Miranda told her. She turned to the others. "Chloe would like to be out in the big world," she said.

"I wouldn't want to end up giving donkey rides on the beach like you did, Mother," Chloe said.

"What would you like to do then?" Caravan Bear asked.

Chloe thought. "I'd like to be famous," she said at last.

That gave Christopher Rabbit an idea. "Would you like me to tell you a story from the Bible after we've had supper?" he asked. "The story has a donkey in it and I think you'll like it, Chloe."

After supper, Christopher Rabbit went out onto the caravan's steps. He saw that all the donkeys in the sanctuary were wandering over toward the caravan. They stopped and looked up at him expectantly. He would have a large audience, he thought, but this wouldn't be as scary as the time he had read a story from the Bible at a safari park in front of a lot of very frightening animals like lions and tigers.***

He opened his Bible and began. "Jesus, who was God's son, had spent around three years on his travels across the country, telling people the good news about God. They had seen him help the poor, heal the sick, and perform miracles. Word had spread and people who lived in towns and villages miles away wanted to see him."

"He'd become famous, had he?" Chloe asked.

"Yes. Everyone had heard about him. Now, after years of travels, God told him to go to Jerusalem, the most important city in the country."

"Wasn't that where he went to the Passover festival, when his parents lost him?" asked Caravan Bear.

"Yes. He was twelve years old then. He was now about thirty-three. So he and his disciples – "

"What are disciples?" Whitby interrupted.

"They were Jesus' friends, who believed in him and tried to follow his teaching. As they walked toward the city, he sent two of them off to a nearby village. He told them that when they entered the village, they would find a donkey and a young colt tied up. He said they should untie them and if anyone asked what they were doing, they were to say that the Lord needed them and they would be returned."

"How did he know the donkey and the colt would be there?" Miranda asked.

"God probably told him," Caravan Bear replied.

"Didn't the donkeys' owner think Jesus' friends were stealing them?" asked Whitby.

"The owner asked why they were untying the donkeys and they replied that the Master needed them," Christopher Rabbit replied. "Jesus' friends threw their cloaks over the backs of the animals and brought them to Jesus. He mounted the colt and set off for Jerusalem."

"What about the donkey, the colt's mother?" Chloe asked. "Was she left behind?"

"The donkey went along too," Christopher Rabbit replied.

"She might have gone in case the colt was frightened," Miranda said gently. "The first time carrying a person on your back can feel a bit odd. Perhaps the colt had never been ridden before. And there would have been a lot of people in a city," she added.

Chloe tossed her head. "I wouldn't like you to come with me," she said to her mother. "I wouldn't be frightened of crowds."

"You might have been scared of *these* crowds," Christopher Rabbit said. "As Jesus and his twelve friends entered Jerusalem, more and more people gathered and walked behind them. There were crowds in front as well, lining the streets, hanging out of windows, standing on the roofs of houses. They cheered, they shouted, they poured blessings on him, they called him the Messiah – the saviour, promised by God."

"Was he as famous as a pop star?" asked Chloe, her eyes wide.

"Or a footballer?" asked another donkey.

"Or someone on television?" asked a third.

Christopher Rabbit nodded. "More famous than all of them."

Chloe sighed. "I'd love that," she said.

"Hold on a minute," said Hector. "If Jesus was as famous as that, why did he travel into Jerusalem on a donkey? I mean, no disrespect to donkeys, but as he was the Messiah, shouldn't he have entered Jerusalem in a bit more style – on a horse," he suggested, tossing his mane, "or even a camel?"

Jesus in Jerusalem

The donkeys listening to the story began muttering among themselves and some very unfriendly glances were cast at Hector.

"Many years before Jesus was born, prophets had spoken about a great day when God's Messiah would come to Jerusalem," Christopher Rabbit replied. "He would come, they said, riding on a donkey colt, one who had never been ridden before. That's why Jesus chose to enter Jerusalem on a young donkey. When the people saw him ride in, they knew that their saviour had come. They went wild, spreading their cloaks on the road in front of him, cutting branches from the palm trees in nearby fields to throw before him."

"Why did they do that?" asked Chloe.

"I think it was to smooth the way," said Christopher Rabbit. "I don't suppose they had roads like we have – probably more like dusty tracks with lots of holes in them."

"There are lots of holes in the roads we've taken with the caravan," Hector snorted.

"Not everyone was happy to see Jesus, however. Some of the religious leaders didn't like the way the crowds shouted for him. They were worried about who the people thought he was and how popular he seemed to be."

"Why?" asked Hector.

"Perhaps they saw him as a threat," Caravan Bear wondered.

Christopher Rabbit nodded. "Jesus had often said that the Pharisees did not follow God's way or practise what they taught, even though they were religious leaders. So yes, they did see Jesus as a threat."

"What happened?" asked Whitby.

"Jesus went to the Temple courtyards and looked around, but it was getting late so he left Jerusalem and went back to the village of Bethany with his friends."

"That's a bit of a let-down," said Hector. "Entering Jerusalem with all those crowds cheering him and then just slipping away in the evening. Why didn't he stay in some grand house in the city?"

"Because that wasn't his way," Christopher Rabbit said patiently. "He didn't want to rule people the way kings normally did. He wanted to rule people's hearts, calling them back to God. He wanted them to love God just as God loves us."

"Did the colt and his mother return to the village?" asked Chloe.

"I'm sure they did."

"I think I'd rather have stayed in Jerusalem," she said, disappointed.

Caravan Bear, who had been thinking quietly, suddenly said, "Do you think Jesus liked all the fuss that was made? Did he like being famous?"

"I don't suppose he did, otherwise he wouldn't have left Jerusalem," said Hector.

"I expect he knew that fame doesn't always last," said Christopher Rabbit. "Crowds can be all for you one moment and just as easily turn against you."

"My old master couldn't praise me enough when I first started giving donkey rides on the beach,"

Miranda said. "I was the best donkey he'd ever had, he said. Then he bought another donkey and turned against me overnight."

"Did Jesus go back to Jerusalem?" asked Whitby.

"Oh yes. He went back the next day."

"Perhaps riding the colt again?" asked Chloe.

"Perhaps. This time things were very different. He went back to the courts around the Temple. They had been turned into a huge market. There were stalls full of goods that people were buying and selling. There were money changers and people selling pigeons at high prices to poor people. Jesus was very angry."

"Why?" asked Hector.

"He said, 'This should be a house of prayer for all nations, but it has become a den of robbers and thieves!' He overturned the tables and drove out the people selling goods. Once he'd done that, he healed blind and lame people who came to him.

"When the chief priests and teachers heard what had happened, they began to think of ways to kill Jesus. The whole city was in uproar and they were afraid. That evening Jesus and his disciples left the city again."

Christopher Rabbit closed the Bible. Everyone was quiet.

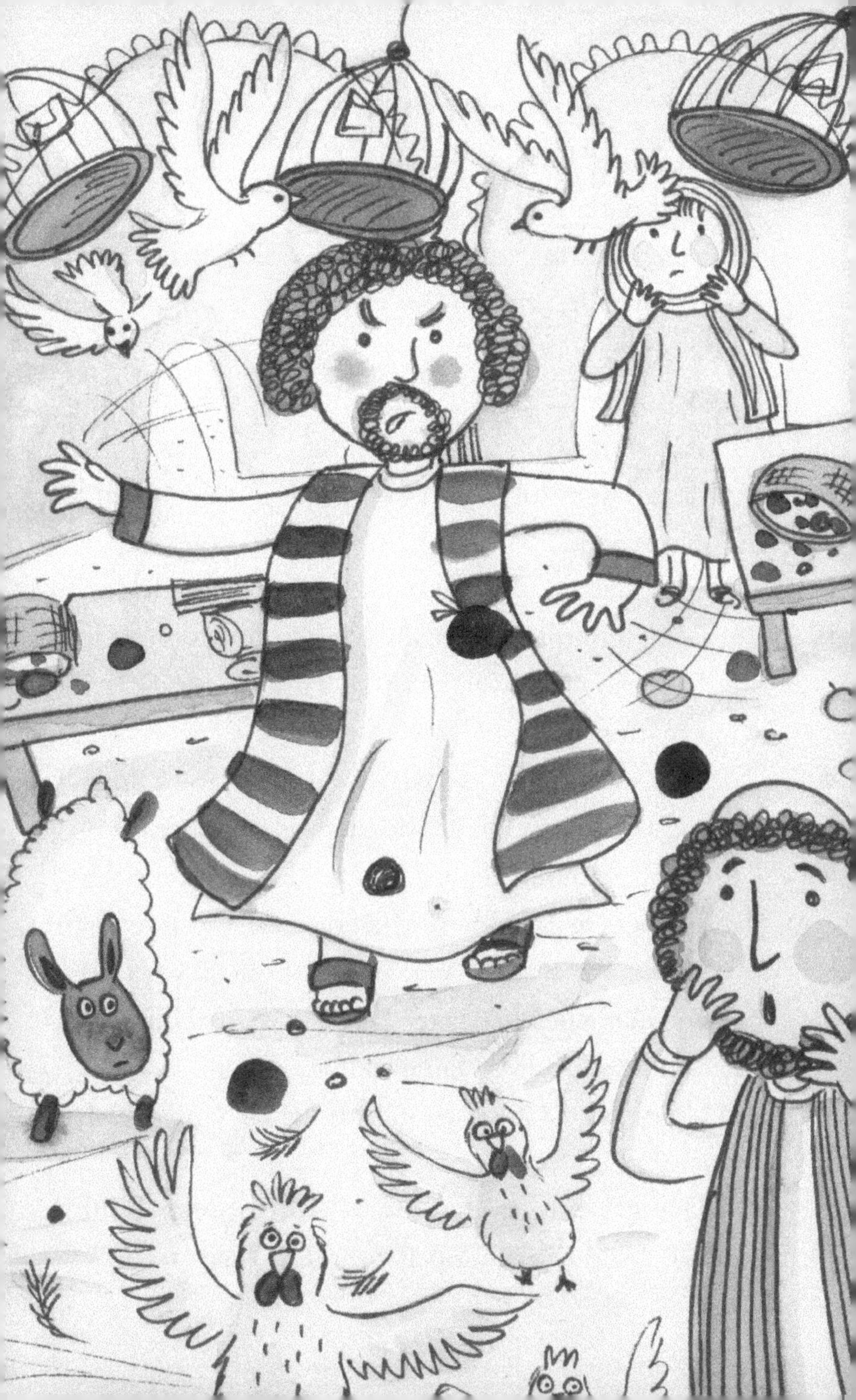

"He must have been very brave to do what he did," Miranda said at last.

"Yes. But he knew he was doing what God wanted and that must have given him strength," said Christopher Rabbit.

The donkeys slowly moved away, Miranda and Chloe last of all.

"I'm so grateful to you for coming," said Miranda. "Do come and visit us again."

Chloe started to walk away, then turned back.

"Being famous isn't really what's important, is it?" she said slowly. "What you're famous for – that's what matters, isn't it?"

"Jesus was famous as a healer, a teacher, and a bringer of God's good news that God loves us and cares for us," Christopher Rabbit replied gently. "He was everything that the people called him when he rode into Jerusalem – yet only a few days later, many of those who were praising him when he entered the city wanted him dead. That's how short-lived fame can be."

"I see," said Chloe thoughtfully. "Thank you for that story."

"Thank God for that story," Christopher Rabbit replied. "And thank God for sending Jesus to us."

Jesus in Jerusalem

Christopher Rabbit watched as Chloe trotted away after her mother.

"Please God, watch over all the animals in this sanctuary and all the animals and people who are looking for somewhere safe to live. And please God, watch over Chloe and Miranda."

Then he went into the caravan and closed the door.

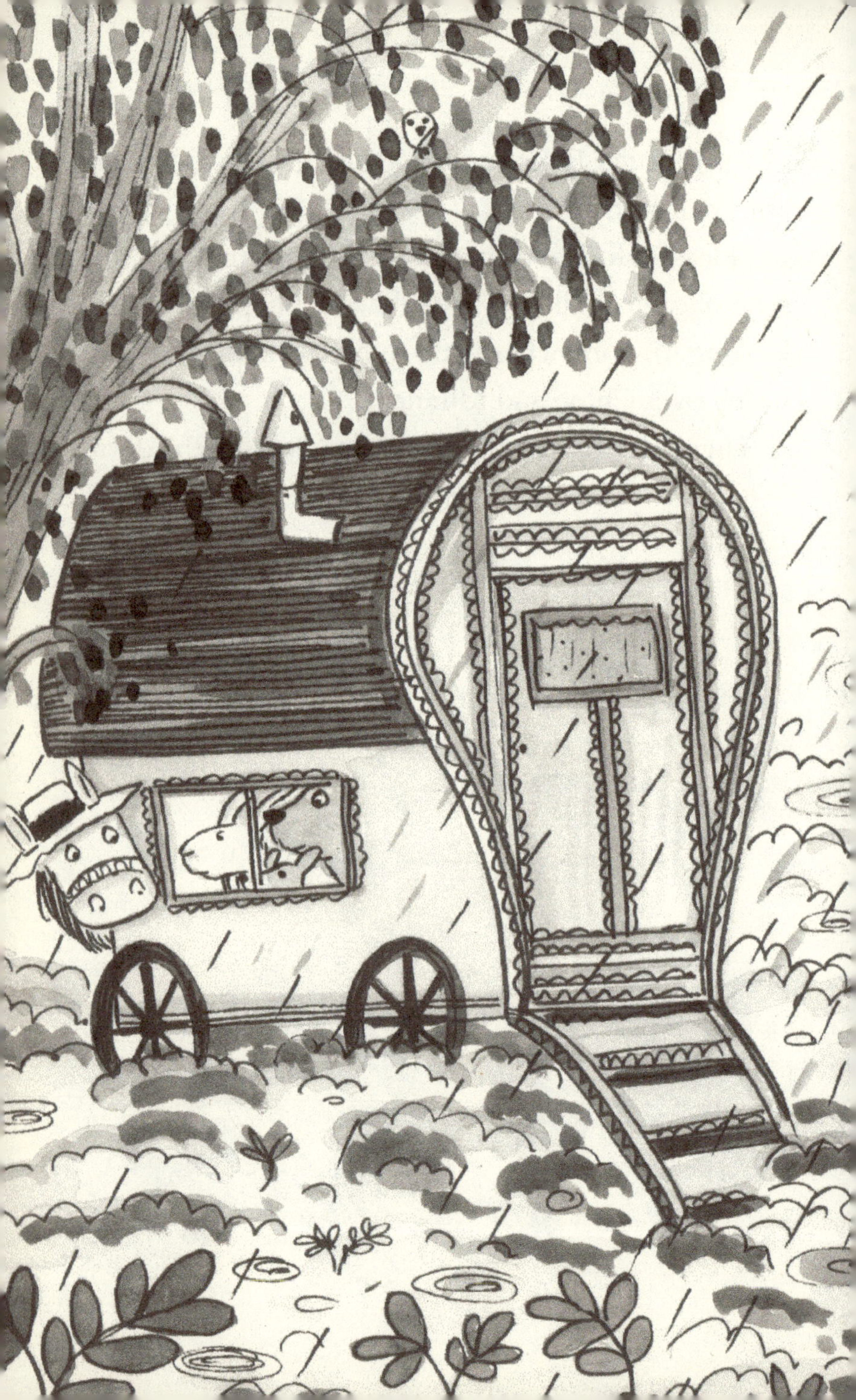

6

The Last Supper

It had been raining for days. Water had been dripping from the trees under which the caravan was parked, and its wheels had sunk deep into the mud.

Caravan Bear, Whitby, and Christopher Rabbit had found it fun to begin with, squelching through paths and jumping up and down in the puddles, but now they sat glumly in the caravan watching raindrops slide down the window.

Whitby sighed. "I'm bored."

"It's all right for you," grumbled Hector, who was standing dejectedly outside the caravan, rain dripping off the end of his nose. "You're nice and dry."

"You could come inside," Whitby suggested.

"I couldn't. I wouldn't get in through the door."

"I'll pull you, and Caravan Bear and Christopher Rabbit can push."

"No, thank you. I'd get stuck."

"No, you wouldn't!"

"Yes, I would."

"You wouldn't!"

"I would, and I'm not going to try it," said Hector firmly. "I'd rather stay out here and get wet."

"Well, stop grumbling, then," snapped Whitby.

"I'm not grumbling," Hector retorted. "I'm just saying that you're in the dry and I'm in the wet. And you're the one who's grumbling."

"Would you like to play a game?" asked Caravan Bear, trying to stop the argument.

No one answered. Whitby continued to look out of the window while Christopher Rabbit picked up his Bible and began reading by himself.

Caravan Bear sighed. "Shall I make a nice supper and ask some of the woodland animals to join us?" he suggested. "They must find it pretty miserable outside."

Hector nodded in agreement. "It *is* pretty miserable outside."

"I'll help with the cooking," said Christopher Rabbit, closing his book.

But before they could begin, they heard the distant sound of a horn and a whoosh of tyres. Caravan Bear peered out.

"That sounds like…" he began.

"Runt!" Whitby groaned.

A moment later there was a squeal of brakes and a motorbike skidded on the wet leaves, narrowly missing crashing into the caravan. Runt, the large pink pig who was riding it, fell off with a loud thump. He got up and beamed around at the animals.

"Lovely weather we're having!"

"Are you all right?" Christopher Rabbit asked.

"Fine! I fall off the bike all the time."

"It was a narrow escape," commented Hector.

"Narrow escape? Huh! You should see some of the narrow escapes I've had. That was nothing!"

"I was thinking about the caravan," Hector murmured.

Runt took off his crash helmet and entered the caravan, shaking himself. Raindrops spattered Caravan Bear, Christopher Rabbit, and Whitby, and dripped on to the floor.

"I bet you didn't expect to see me, did you?" Runt asked.

"No, I can't say we did," Caravan Bear said politely.

"How are May and Maytwo?" asked Christopher Rabbit. They were Runt's twin daughters.

"They're fine! Might have come with me, only we wouldn't all fit on the bike," Runt explained.

"Would you like to stay for supper?" Caravan Bear asked. "I was just about to make it."

"Supper and a story," Runt said briskly. "Couldn't be better!"

A very wet hedgehog, a squirrel with a muddy tail, a bedraggled bat, and a shivering dormouse joined them. They were glad to get dry and ate a hearty meal. After every crumb had been eaten, Christopher Rabbit got out his Bible and opened it.

"Jesus had entered Jerusalem just before the festival of Passover. Crowds had welcomed him. But he knew he was in danger from the religious leaders who wanted to kill him," Christopher Rabbit explained to their guests

"Why did they want to kill him?" asked the squirrel, who was nibbling a nut.

"They were jealous of him because he was popular," Whitby said. "He was as popular as a pop star." She thought for a moment. "More popular."

Runt swelled with pride. "I'm popular with the farmer," he said. "He likes me so much that he lent me his motorbike. 'Runtie,' he said. 'Runtie, I have you to thank for the successful pig farm I run.'"

No one replied to this.

"They thought Jesus was a threat," Caravan Bear explained.

"Yes," agreed Christopher Rabbit. "He was known throughout the land as a great prophet and healer and people were calling him the messiah, the saviour sent by God, the one everyone had been waiting for."

"He was God's son as well as all those other names, wasn't he?" asked Whitby.

Christopher Rabbit nodded.

"Must have been an awful responsibility, being God's son," said Hector, shaking his head.

"I wonder if *I'm* God's son?" Runt said thoughtfully. "I must be as popular as Jesus was."

"Have you made as many enemies?" Hector asked.

"Oh, one or two," Runt said airily. "Not many. I like people to like me."

"I don't think Jesus worried about people liking him," said Christopher Rabbit. "He wasn't worried about being popular either. He just wanted to show people what God was like so that they would try to follow God's way by loving one another."

"Loving one another is all very nice but it doesn't get you anywhere," Runt said firmly. "I couldn't run the pig farm if I were nice."

"I thought it was the farmer's farm, not yours," Whitby said.

Runt grinned. "He thinks it's his farm but I make all the important decisions."

The Last Supper

"If the religious leaders wanted to kill Jesus, why didn't he run away?" asked the dormouse. "I would have."

"He was brave, that's why," said Caravan Bear.

"I've never run away from trouble," Runt said importantly. "Running away gets you nowhere."

"It gets you somewhere safe," Hector murmured.

Christopher Rabbit thought it high time he went on with the story. "It was time for Jesus and the disciples to prepare for the Passover meal," he began firmly.

"That was when the Israelites remembered how God had saved them from slavery in Egypt," Caravan Bear explained to those who didn't know the story.*

"A man had promised Jesus a room where they could eat the Passover meal in safety," Christopher Rabbit continued. "So Jesus sent Peter and John ahead of the others, telling them that when they entered Jerusalem, they should follow a man carrying a jar of water."

"Weren't there lots of men walking around carrying water jars?" Caravan Bear asked. "How would they know which was the right one?"

Christopher Rabbit shook his head. "I think they'd know because carrying water was usually done by women. Jesus said that the man would lead them to a house and the owner would show them to an upstairs room where they could have their meal."

"Was it dangerous for Jesus to walk through the city in the daylight?" asked the squirrel.

"Probably."

"That's why bats fly at night," said the bat. "Safer and better for hunting."

"Shall I go on?" asked Christopher Rabbit. Without waiting for an answer, he continued. "Peter and John found the room and began preparing the meal. Jesus arrived later with the rest of his disciples."

"Who were they?" asked Hector.

"Let's see." Christopher Rabbit looked it up in the Bible. "There was Simon, who Jesus called Peter, and his brother, Andrew. There were another two brothers, James and John. Then there was Philip, Bartholomew, Thomas, Matthew, another James, Thaddaeus, another Simon, and Judas Iscariot."

"That makes twelve," said Runt confidently. "I'm good at counting."

"As the disciples arrived, they looked around for someone to come and wash their feet – "

"Why did they do that?" the squirrel interrupted.

"I think it was the custom for a servant to wash the feet of guests," Christopher Rabbit replied. "Jesus got up, wrapped a towel around his waist, poured water into a basin, and began to wash his disciples' feet. Then he dried them with the towel."

"But Jesus wasn't a servant," Caravan Bear protested.

"No, he wasn't. He was their master. Peter was horrified when Jesus did that and all of them felt uncomfortable. It just didn't seem right."

"Hold on a minute," Runt said. "If Jesus washed everyone's feet, which I think was an unnecessary thing for him to do – you wouldn't catch me washing the pigs' trotters, especially after they've been rooting around in the mud – but if Jesus washed his disciples' feet, who washed Jesus' feet?"

There was silence.

"I don't suppose anyone did," Christopher Rabbit said.

"That's a pity," said Whitby. "His feet must have been as dirty as everyone else's."

"Perhaps he washed his own feet," Hector suggested.

"When Jesus had finished, he returned to his place at the table," Christopher Rabbit continued. "He told his disciples that if he, as their Lord and teacher, could act as a servant and wash their feet, then they should be prepared to wash each other's feet. They must be servants to each other."

"And did they?" asked the dormouse, round-eyed.

"What?" asked Christopher Rabbit.

"Wash each other's feet."

"Of course they didn't," said Hector scornfully. "Jesus had just done it!"

"I do think someone should have washed Jesus' feet," said the bat worriedly.

"Do you think we should wash our feet?" asked the hedgehog.

"Or wash each other's?" added the bat.

"I think that what Jesus meant," Christopher Rabbit explained patiently, "was that he was willing to do anything for them, even wash their feet. He did it because he loved them.

"They began eating and then Jesus told them that one of them would give him away to his enemies. His friends looked at one another. One by one they asked Jesus who it would be. Jesus dipped a piece of bread into a dish of food and told them that the person sharing the food with him would be the one who would betray him."

"Which one was it?" asked Whitby breathlessly.

"I think it was... Thadd... whatever his name was," said the squirrel.

"Why?" asked the bat.

"I don't like the name and can't pronounce it."

"Well, I think it was Simon, who was called Peter," said the hedgehog. "Changing your name sounds suspicious to me."

"Jesus had changed it for him," said Christopher Rabbit mildly.

"Why did he do that?"

"I can't remember."

"Is this a guessing game?" asked Hector.

Christopher Rabbit shook his head. "It was Judas Iscariot. He was the man who looked after the disciples' money and he had promised the Jewish

The Last Supper

leaders that he would tell them where to find Jesus in return for thirty pieces of silver."

"I was going to say him next," said the squirrel with a satisfied air. "I don't like his name either."

"That was a terrible thing to do," Whitby exclaimed. "Why did he do it? Was it for the money?"

"People do really bad things for money," Hector said wisely. "I'm glad I don't have any."

Christopher Rabbit shrugged. "Perhaps. Or it might have been that Jesus wasn't the sort of leader Judas had hoped he'd be."

"What do you mean?" asked the squirrel.

"The country was ruled by the Romans. Judas might have thought that if Jesus was really the saviour sent by God, he would lead an army to defeat the Romans and throw them out. Instead – "

" – instead, Jesus didn't behave like a king at all, did he?" Caravan Bear interrupted.

"No," Christopher Rabbit said slowly. "He didn't."

"What did Judas do?" asked the bat.

"He left the room and went out into the night," said Christopher Rabbit.

He was silent for a moment.

"And Jesus didn't stop him?" Caravan Bear asked.

Christopher Rabbit shook his head.

"Didn't any of the other disciples stop him?" asked the hedgehog.

"I don't think they truly understood what Jesus meant," Christopher Rabbit said.

"Well, they all must have been stupid, then," Runt declared. "Didn't you say Jesus told them that the person who shared his food would betray him?"

"Yes."

"Perhaps they were tired," the dormouse said. He yawned. "I must admit I'm getting a bit sleepy too, although I'm really enjoying the story."

"What happened after Judas left?" asked the squirrel.

"They went on with their meal," said Christopher Rabbit.

"Even though Jesus knew that Judas would betray him?" asked Runt.

Christopher Rabbit nodded. "Jesus took a loaf of bread, thanked God for it, and passed it to the others. 'This is my body,' he said. 'I'm going to be broken, like this bread. I am going to die, for all of you and for everyone.'

"Then he took a cup of wine and thanked God for it before sharing it around. 'This is my blood,' he said, 'which, like this wine, will be shed. Remember this night and when you share bread and wine in future, remember that my death will make our peace with God for ever.'"

Runt shook his head. "I don't understand."

"Neither did his disciples," said Christopher Rabbit.

"What did Jesus mean?" asked Hector, mystified.

"I'm not altogether sure," Christopher Rabbit said cautiously. "But I think that when God made the world and everything in it, he made everyone free. People were free to be good and kind and follow God. Or free to be cruel and make a mess of the world. But people often didn't follow God. It wasn't that they didn't believe in him, they just didn't pay him much attention."

"I've never paid much attention to God," said Runt. "And he's never paid much attention to me."

"How do you know that?" asked Whitby.

Runt looked stubborn but said nothing.

"I think God pays attention to everyone," said Christopher Rabbit. "And because he loves us, he sent his son, Jesus, to remind people about him. Many people who saw Jesus and listened to what he had to say chose to turn to God and love and obey him.

"But some of them, like the religious leaders, were frightened of him and wanted to kill him. Jesus knew that his death was part of God's great plan. He knew that if he was prepared to die for all the wrongs people had done, everyone could share in God's forgiveness."

He stopped and it grew very quiet in the caravan.

"It's very late," said the hedgehog.

"Time I was off," said the squirrel.

One by one, the animals said goodnight and left the caravan. Runt put on his crash helmet.

"Must go," he said. "The farmer might be missing his bike."

The Last Supper

"I thought he lent it to you," said Caravan Bear.

"Well, yes, he did. In a manner of speaking." Runt hesitated a moment. "Will you come to the farm and go on with the story?" he asked.

"If you like."

Runt nodded, climbed onto the bike, and roared off into the dark.

"I hope he's all right," said Christopher Rabbit. He went to the door and peered outside.

The rain had stopped and it was a clear night with a full, bright moon.

"Please, God, help Runt get home safely without having an accident. And thank you for the story of Jesus' last supper with his friends. Thank you for what he did for all of us. We know how much you love us and that you always offer to forgive us when we do wrong."

Then he closed the door of the caravan and went to bed.

In the Garden

As Hector towed the caravan along the road leading to the pig farm, two pigs came running to meet him. They turned out to be May and Maytwo.

"You can't stay on the farm," May gasped, out of breath.

"Why not?" Caravan Bear asked, jumping down from the steps. "The farmer has always let us stay here before."

"Well, he won't now," said Maytwo. "Dad said to tell you to go on to the farm further up the road."

"Dad's not in the farmer's good books," said May, giggling.

In the Garden

"Not since he crashed his motorbike," Maytwo explained.

"Is your dad all right?" Hector asked.

"Oh, he's fine," said May, dismissively. "Just cuts and bruises."

"The motorbike isn't, though," Maytwo added. "It's completely broken."

"We'll see you later," said May. "We told Dad we'd come and hear the story so we can tell him about it."

"It's a real bore, but he made us promise," May explained.

"And you know what Dad's like," Maytwo went on.

"EMBARRASSING!" they said together and walked off, squealing with laughter.

Christopher Rabbit, Caravan Bear, Whitby, and Hector looked at each other.

"I never thought I'd feel sorry for Runt," said Whitby, jumping up the steps of the caravan.

A short while later, Hector stopped beside a large notice that read "Jubbly's Farm and Garden Centre".

"What's a 'garden centre'"? asked Whitby.

"It's a place where they sell plants and things for the garden," said Caravan Bear.

At that moment a very fine black cockerel with brilliant red-brown neck feathers and a bright red crest stalked up to them.

"If you are the caravan sent by the pig, you are expected," said the cockerel in a grand voice. "Follow me."

Without waiting for their reply, he walked off. Hector followed meekly.

The cockerel led them into a walled garden filled with row after row of potted trees and plants.

"You can park over there," he said, waving a wing. "Make sure you park with the caravan neatly against the wall, facing outward. We have strict rules here. Mr Jubbly cannot abide a mess." He stared at them in a disapproving way. "Neither can I."

"Thank you," said Caravan Bear meekly. "And please thank Mr Jubbly."

The cockerel puffed out his chest.

"As Mr Jubbly's steward, I am responsible for the farm and garden centre. If you need anything, you can ask for me at the farm. My name is Nathan."

With that, he gave a loud crow and proudly stalked away.

In the Garden

"Well!" said Hector.

"How does he know Runt?" wondered Caravan Bear as he unhitched the horse.

"This is an odd place," said Whitby, jumping down from the caravan and running off. A moment later she was back.

"Look!" she whispered. "Over there! There are lots and lots of funny little people!"

The others looked around.

Standing stiffly in straight rows were neatly painted figures, all with long beards and bright hats. They seemed to be staring at the caravan.

For a moment no one said anything, then Caravan Bear laughed.

"They're garden gnomes," he said.

"Do you think they mind us being here?" Whitby whispered anxiously.

"They're not real," Christopher Rabbit assured her. "People buy them to put in their gardens."

Whitby wasn't convinced until she had run over to them and barked loudly in their painted faces.

By the time they had eaten, it was growing dark. Christopher Rabbit picked up his Bible.

"Do you think May and Maytwo are coming?" asked Caravan Bear.

"Here they are," said Hector as the two pigs arrived.

"Who are all those little people?" Maytwo asked.

"Only garden gnomes," said Christopher Rabbit patiently. "They won't hurt you."

May pushed one of the gnomes, which promptly fell down.

"Pick that up this minute!" came a loud voice. Nathan, the cockerel, was entering the garden.

May picked up the gnome.

"Put it back in the right place!" said Nathan sternly.

May gulped and replaced the gnome.

"Young animals these days – no sense of order or discipline," Nathan sighed.

"How is your father?" Hector asked the pigs politely.

"Oh, you know…" said May.

In the Garden

"EMBARRASSING!" said Maytwo and they both laughed loudly.

Nathan muttered something about the young having no manners.

"Would you like me to start?" Christopher Rabbit asked politely. Everyone settled down.

"After supper, Jesus talked to his friends as they walked to a garden on the outskirts of Jerusalem," Christopher Rabbit read. "He told them what was going to happen to him and said that they would all run away and leave him. Peter replied that he would never leave Jesus, but Jesus told him that before the cockerel had crowed twice at dawn the following morning, Peter would have said three times that he didn't know him. Peter thought that was ridiculous. He said he would never leave Jesus. He would rather die with him. The other disciples said the same."

Nathan nodded his magnificent head. "Not the thing to abandon your friends," he said approvingly.

"When they reached the garden, which was called Gethsemane, Jesus took three of his friends with him and the other disciples sat down to wait. Jesus was very upset. 'Don't go,' he said to Peter, James, and John. 'Keep me company.'

"They entered a grove of trees and Jesus knelt down to pray. 'Please, Father, save me from this terrible death. Rescue me, if it's possible. But only if that's what *you* want – not what I want.'"

"And did God rescue him?" Whitby asked anxiously.

"Wait and see," said Caravan Bear.

"Jesus stopped praying and looked around for his friends," Christopher Rabbit continued.

"I bet they'd run away," said May.

"No, they hadn't," Christopher Rabbit said. "They'd fallen asleep."

"Fine friends," Nathan murmured.

"They were probably tired," said Caravan Bear peaceably.

"Probably," Christopher Rabbit agreed. "Jesus woke them, but once he began to pray again, they went back to sleep."

"Well, it must have been pretty boring for them," Maytwo said. "Just sitting in the garden with nothing to do while Jesus was praying."

"Boring," May agreed, nodding her head.

"Couldn't they have played a game while they were waiting?" Whitby asked.

"You don't suddenly start playing a game in the middle of the night in the middle of a garden when your friend and teacher is upset and waiting for his enemies to come and kill him," said Caravan Bear sternly. "It wouldn't be a very nice thing to do, would it?"

"What sort of a game do you think they'd play anyway?" asked Hector sarcastically. "Football?"

"All right," said Whitby. "I only wondered."

"Jesus woke them for a third time," Christopher Rabbit went on. "'Couldn't you stay awake, even for an hour?' he asked them sadly.

"Just then a large crowd arrived. They were led by Judas. Behind him were the chief priests, who had come with guards carrying swords and stout clubs.

"Judas had been one of Jesus' friends and was going to betray him," Caravan Bear explained to the newcomers.

"For thirty pieces of silver," Whitby added.

"Judas walked straight up to Jesus," Christopher Rabbit continued. "'Hello, Master!' he said, and kissed him."

"Why did he do that?" asked May.

"Judas had told the priests that the man they should arrest would be the one he kissed. The guards grabbed hold of Jesus, treating him as if he was a dangerous criminal. Jesus' friends were furious. Peter drew his sword and lashed out, cutting off the ear of one of the high priest's servants. Jesus stopped him from doing any more damage. He touched the wounded ear and it was healed."

"Wow!" said Whitby. "Was that a miracle?"

Christopher Rabbit nodded.

"Then what happened?" Whitby asked.

"Jesus' friends ran away."

Nathan snorted. "Well, I call that a very poor show. Falling asleep then running away! A very poor show indeed!"

"I suppose they were frightened. It was the end of all their hopes and I imagine they just panicked," said Christopher Rabbit. "Anyway, Jesus was arrested and taken to the house of Caiaphas, the high priest. The chief priests had decided to put Jesus on trial straight away, even though it must have been quite late."

"Why were they in such a hurry?" asked Hector.

"Perhaps they were afraid of what the crowds might do if they heard about it," Christopher Rabbit said. He went on. "Although Peter and another friend had run off, they hadn't gone far. When

Who Jesus Was

they saw Jesus being taken away, they followed the soldiers to Caiaphas's house.

"They went into the courtyard to see what would happen to Jesus. There was a fire burning and a group of servants were standing nearby. It was a cold night. Peter joined them, warming his hands. A servant girl stared at him. 'You were with Jesus, that man from Nazareth. You're one of his disciples,' she said. Peter was scared. 'I don't know what you're talking about,'

In the Garden

he replied. Just then a cockerel crowed."

"Must have been nearly morning," said Nathan. "Cockerels are excellent timekeepers. We're up early and crow before dawn." He thought for a minute. "You could say we're reliable as clockwork." He puffed out his chest feathers.

Christopher Rabbit continued. "A man peered at Peter. 'You're one of that lot!' he said. 'I'm not!' Peter insisted. A little while later another man came up to him. 'You *are* one of them. I can tell by your accent.' Peter lost his temper. 'I don't know that man. You're talking rubbish!' he shouted. At that moment the cockerel crowed for the second time and Peter remembered what Jesus had said to him."

"That Peter would deny knowing Jesus three times before the cockerel had crowed twice," said Hector.

"What did Peter do?" asked Whitby.

"He burst into tears and ran away," said Christopher Rabbit.

"Those friends of Jesus weren't very brave," Nathan said disapprovingly.

"It must have been very frightening for Jesus' friends," Caravan Bear said mildly.

"Must have been even more frightening for Jesus," said Hector.

"I'd have run away," said Whitby. "But then I'm not very brave."

May and Maytwo had been whispering and giggling at the start of the story but now they were quiet.

"Do you think Jesus was scared?" Maytwo asked suddenly.

"I don't know," said Christopher Rabbit. "Probably. However, he did know he was doing what God wanted – and maybe that gave him strength, and he trusted that God would be with him whatever happened."

He looked down at the Bible and went on. "The men holding Jesus began to make fun of him. They blindfolded him and beat him before taking him before the council of important religious people. Some people came forward and told lies about Jesus, but they couldn't prove anything against him.

"At last, the high priest challenged Jesus. 'Are you the Messiah, the Son of God?' he asked. Jesus replied, 'You say that I am.'"

"Mmm," said Nathan, "that's a very clever answer."

In the Garden

"Why?" asked Hector.

"Because he doesn't say he was the Son of God," explained Nathan.

"Oh, I see," Hector said, nodding his head and trying to look wise.

"And he doesn't say he wasn't."

"Oh. I don't think I *do* see," said Hector, looking confused.

Christopher Rabbit continued. "The high priest asked the council for their verdict. 'He deserves death,' they replied."

"That's not a proper trial," said Nathan severely. "Held in the middle of the night, without anyone to defend him. I don't agree with that."

"So did they kill him there and then?" asked May.

"No," Christopher Rabbit replied. "Early in the morning they took Jesus to the Roman governor, Pilate. As the Romans ruled the country, they were the only ones who could pass the death sentence. They told Pilate that Jesus had been stirring up trouble and asked that he be put to death. Pilate questioned Jesus but couldn't see that Jesus had done anything wrong."

"Of course he hadn't!" Whitby burst out, quite upset. "All Jesus did was tell people about God and how God cares for everyone. And he was kind and good!"

"I know," said Christopher Rabbit. "While this was happening, crowds of people began arriving. Stirred up by the religious leaders, they were shouting, 'Crucify him!'"

"What does that mean?" asked Maytwo.

"It was one of the ways in which Romans put people to death," Christopher Rabbit explained. "They nailed them to a wooden cross."

"I've always said people can be very cruel," said Hector, shaking his head. "My old master often beat me for no reason at all."

"During the festival of Passover, it was the custom for one prisoner to be set free by the Roman governor," Christopher Rabbit went on. "Pilate, knowing that Jesus was innocent, asked the crowd if they wanted Jesus to be released or a murderer called Barabbas. The crowd shouted for Barabbas.

"Pilate didn't know what to do, but because he was afraid of the people, he decided to wash his hands of the whole thing. 'It's your affair, not mine,' he said, and handed Jesus over to the soldiers to be put to death as the crowd demanded."

In the Garden

"That was a cowardly thing to do," said Nathan. "If he knew Jesus was innocent, Pilate should have released him."

"Why didn't he?" Hector asked.

"He might have been frightened of a full-scale riot," Christopher Rabbit replied.

"That's all very well, but the Romans could have put a stop to a riot, couldn't they?" Hector objected. "After all, they were in charge and had all those well-trained soldiers. To say nothing of those well-trained horses," he added.

Christopher Rabbit nodded. "He was probably afraid of losing his job as governor." He went on. "The Roman soldiers took Jesus and whipped him. They made a crown of thorns and put it on his head.

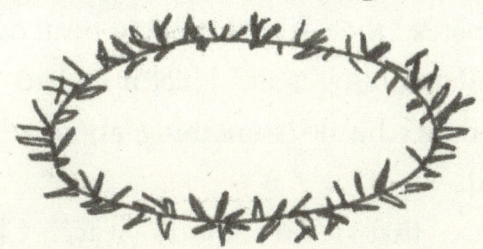

'Hail, King of the Jews,' they said, making fun of him. Then they led him away to crucify him."

Christopher Rabbit stopped reading. It was quite dark now in the garden. For a moment no one spoke.

"I don't understand," Caravan Bear said at last. "Didn't those crowds cheer Jesus just a few days before, when he entered Jerusalem on a donkey?"

"Yes."

"So why did they change their minds so quickly?"

Christopher Rabbit shrugged. "I don't know. Perhaps the people were convinced by the lies that they were told about Jesus. Perhaps they were afraid of the Romans and didn't want to upset them."

"I wonder if the people were disappointed," Caravan Bear said. "They might have thought, like Judas, that if Jesus was really the Messiah, God's son, he would have come with a great army and thrown the Romans out of their country."

"And instead they saw him being beaten and made fun of, and accepting it all," Hector added.

"Why didn't he do something about it?" Nathan demanded.

"Because that wasn't God's way," Christopher Rabbit replied. "Jesus said that God loves us and wants us to love each other."

There was silence for a moment in the garden.

"What happened to Judas?" Whitby asked suddenly.

In the Garden

Christopher Rabbit turned a page in his Bible. "When he'd led the guards to the garden and pointed out Jesus, he suddenly realized just what he had done. He was sorry, terribly sorry. He rushed to the Temple.

"'Jesus is innocent,' he cried. 'I've done a dreadful thing!' The priests and elders shrugged. 'That's your problem,' they said. Judas threw down the money he'd been paid, went away, and killed himself."

The animals were quiet.

"I'm glad he was sorry for what he'd done," Whitby said at last.

"Bit late," said Hector.

"What happened then? To Jesus, I mean?" May asked in a small voice.

"He was crucified," Christopher Rabbit answered.

"And that's the end, is it?" asked Maytwo.

"No," Christopher Rabbit replied. "That's not the end at all. But it's late and I think I should read what happened next another day."

He stood up and stretched.

"We were going to start going home tomorrow – " Caravan Bear began.

"You can't do that!" said May.

"You've got to finish the story," Maytwo added. "We'll tell Dad what you've just told us but he'll be very angry if he doesn't hear the end."

"And you haven't seen Dad when he's angry," May said, grinning. She pulled a face, looked at her sister, and together they said, "EMBARRASSING!" They laughed, and went off.

Nathan watched them go with a disapproving expression on his face. "If my chicks acted like that, they'd soon get a peck or two from me to teach them how to behave."

"Might we stay here an extra night?" asked Caravan Bear.

Nathan nodded his head in a grand manner.

In the Garden

"Of course," he said. "I must confess to feeling some curiosity myself about what happened. After all, once Jesus had been killed, he was dead, wasn't he?"

With that he stalked off in a stately fashion.

Christopher Rabbit watched him walk away, the cockerel's head held high and his bright tail feathers quivering.

"Thank you, God, for sending us Jesus, to show us what you are really like. I'm sorry he had to suffer and I'm sorry for his friends who ran away and betrayed him. Help us to be brave and loving to everyone, no matter how unkind and cruel they might be."

"And God, I want to pray that Runt gets better soon and that the farmer isn't too angry with him," Whitby added, which surprised the others, as Whitby wasn't a fan of Runt.

"Well, if we're praying for others, I want to thank God for May and Maytwo," said Hector. "They make me laugh."

"And thank you for Nathan," Caravan Bear added.

"And everyone we've met on our travels," said Christopher Rabbit.

With that, they went into the caravan and fell fast asleep.

8

The Empty Tomb

Whitby, who had been wandering around the garden centre, rushed back to the caravan.

"Look! Come and see this!"

"Look at what?" asked Hector. "If it's any more of those gnomes, I don't want to see them. The ones over by that wall keep looking at me as if they don't like me."

"It's outside! On the road!"

Hector, Caravan Bear, and Christopher Rabbit followed Whitby to the entrance, where they stopped and stared.

Coming up the road was a rusty old tractor. It was being driven by a tall, thin man with a red face and a long nose. He was wearing a battered hat and a well-worn green jacket. Behind him stood a short plump lady. She was wearing a tightly fitting dress patterned

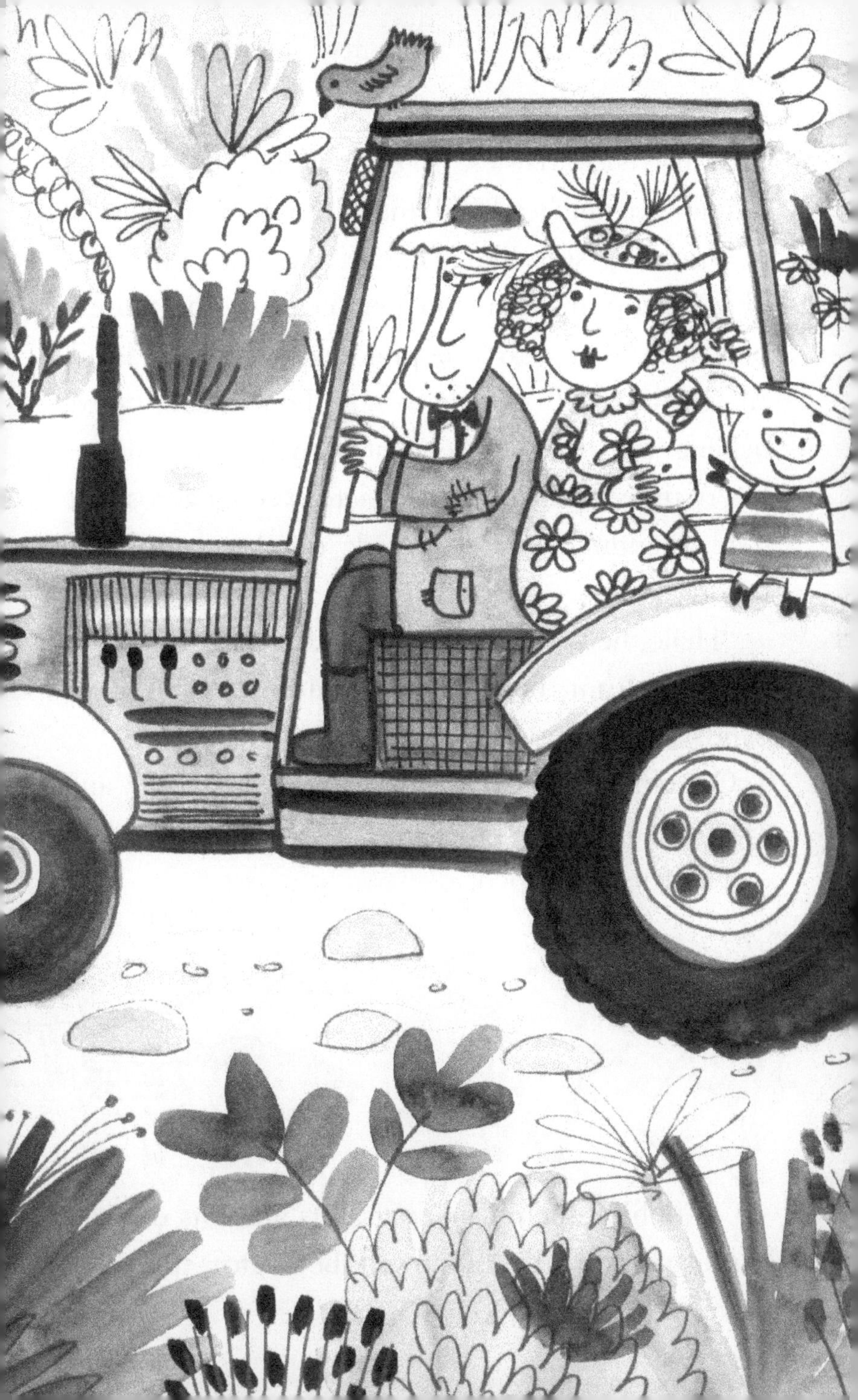

with big yellow daisies. An evening bag studded with sequins was in her hand and the sequins flashed in the morning sun. Fluffy mauve slippers with bright blue pom-poms were on her feet and she wore a pink velvet hat with long pink feathers on her head. As she looked from side to side the feathers waved, tickling the man's nose, which made him sneeze. Every time he sneezed, the tractor veered across the road. Standing beside the lady on the tractor, the friends saw...

"Hello, hello!" came a delighted voice.

It was Runt, beaming as usual despite the large bandage tied around his head.

On either side of the tractor walked May and Maytwo, and behind them...

The friends gasped.

Behind them came pigs, lots and lots of pigs. Large and small, they followed the tractor, spreading out across the road, grunting and squealing.

"Once we told Dad the story, everyone wanted to hear the end," called an excited Maytwo.

"Even the farmer and his wife," May added.

"I don't know what Mr Jubbly will say about this," sniffed Nathan, looking disapprovingly down his beak.

Flying overhead was a flock of pigeons.

"We heard the story and want to hear the end!" called the first pigeon.

The tractor swerved suddenly and drove into the garden centre, narrowly missing hitting the wall. It came to an abrupt stop and the farmer and his wife climbed down.

"Are you all right, Runt?" asked Caravan Bear as the pig climbed out cautiously. They saw that he had another bandage, this one around his leg.

"Right as rain," said Runt. "Ouch!" he squealed as his bad leg hit the side of the tractor. "Had to come by tractor after I had the accident with the motorbike," he explained, and the farmer grunted.

"Follow me, pigs!" Nathan commanded, somewhat late as the pigs had already flooded in through the entrance and were heading toward the walled garden. "Keep in order now and don't disturb the plants!"

"Or the gnomes," said Hector, snorting with laughter.

The pigeons flew over the wall, swooped down, and settled on the heads of the gnomes.

"Not on the gnomes!" Nathan shouted. The pigeons took no notice.

Christopher Rabbit fetched his Bible and sat on the top step. He looked around. Everyone fell silent and watched him attentively. He began to read.

"When Jesus had been condemned to death he was taken through the streets of Jerusalem, and crowds of shouting, jeering people lined the way. Among the crowds were a few women, close friends of Jesus, who cried as they saw their friend, the teacher they loved, like this. They followed the procession toward Golgotha, the hill where criminals were crucified. Jesus was made to carry a large wooden cross, but when he became too weak, the soldiers found a passer-by to carry it for him.

"Once the procession reached Golgotha, the soldiers nailed Jesus to the cross, lifted it up, and set it in a hole in the ground. Above his head they fixed a sign. It read:

THIS IS THE KING OF THE JEWS

"Jesus prayed: 'Father, forgive them, for they don't know what they are doing.'"

Whitby sniffed.

"On either side of him was a criminal, each one nailed to a cross. 'If you're the Messiah, why don't you save us?' one of them called. But the other one shouted across to him, 'We were wicked and deserve our punishment. This man has done nothing wrong!' And then he turned to Jesus and begged, 'When you come into your kingdom, remember me!'

"Jesus replied, 'I promise that you will be with me today in paradise.' At twelve o'clock, when the sun should have been at its brightest, it suddenly became totally dark. And at three o'clock, Jesus cried out, 'Dear God, I am placing my life in your hands!' Then he died."

Christopher Rabbit stopped reading. There was silence in the garden. No one made a sound.

At last Nathan stirred. "Well, that's all very sad. But if that's the end of the story, you pigeons can now kindly remove yourselves from those gnomes."

"But it's not the end at all," Christopher Rabbit replied.

"Isn't it?"

The Empty Tomb

"No." Christopher Rabbit continued. "After Jesus died, Joseph, a friend of his, asked Pilate if he could take Jesus' body. He wrapped it in a linen cloth and laid it on a stone ledge in a cave tomb in a nearby garden."

"Hadn't all of Jesus' friends run away?" asked May.

"Most had, but the women who had watched Jesus die followed to see where he was being buried. They saw some Roman soldiers help Joseph roll an enormous rock in front of the mouth of the cave to seal it. The soldiers left, leaving a couple on guard."

"Why?" asked Hector.

Christopher Rabbit looked down at the book. "It says here that the chief priests went to Pilate and asked if the tomb could be guarded by soldiers. They told him that Jesus had said that three days after he was killed, he would rise from the dead."

"Impossible," snorted Nathan.

"Surely nothing's impossible for God," said Christopher Rabbit mildly. "Anyway, they asked Pilate to arrange for the tomb to be guarded as they didn't want Jesus' friends to steal his body and make false claims."

"Why would they do that?" demanded Runt.

Christopher Rabbit shrugged. "If people thought that Jesus had risen from the dead, it meant that he really was the Messiah – and all the lies the priests had told about him were wrong. They didn't believe that he really would rise from the dead, but they didn't want to take the chance that his friends might steal his body and then claim that he had risen."

"When you're dead, surely you're dead," Nathan said firmly.

"Do you think they were scared?" Whitby asked suddenly.

"Who?" Christopher Rabbit asked.

"The priests."

"Probably."

"Perhaps, deep down, they knew that they'd done a terrible thing," said Hector.

Christopher Rabbit shrugged. "Who knows. Jesus' body was laid in the tomb on that Friday evening. The next day, Saturday, was the Jewish day of rest. But the day after – "

"Was that Sunday?" asked Nathan, who kept being distracted by the pigeons.

Christopher Rabbit nodded. "Yes. Early on Sunday morning, before it was light, some of the women who were friends of Jesus went to the tomb."

The Empty Tomb

"What about his other friends – didn't they go?" asked Whitby.

"No."

"I expect they were hiding," said Caravan Bear.

"Maybe they thought they'd be arrested and crucified as well," said Runt.

"Do you think his friends had doubts?" asked Hector suddenly.

"About what?" Maytwo asked.

"About Jesus."

"What sort of doubts?" May said.

"About who he was. God's son. I mean, you don't expect God's own son to be killed, do you?" Hector explained.

"Whatever the rest of Jesus' friends thought, it was only a few women who were brave enough to go to the tomb," continued Christopher Rabbit. "They took sweet spices to put on Jesus' body."

"Why did they want to do that?" May asked.

"It was what was done in those days. Oils and spices were rubbed onto people's bodies after they'd died."

"Like frankincense and myrrh, the expensive presents the wise men brought to Jesus when he was born," Whitby added.

Christopher Rabbit carried on. "When the women arrived, they saw that the stone had been rolled away. They went inside but couldn't find Jesus' body. When they came out, they were terrified to see two figures in shining clothes standing in front of them."

"What had happened to the guards?" asked May.

"They were so frightened, they'd fallen flat on their faces."

"Were they angels, those two figures?" Whitby asked.

Christopher Rabbit nodded.

"Those angels seem to get everywhere in these stories," Whitby commented.

"They asked the women why they were looking for the living among the dead," Christopher Rabbit went on. "They told them that Jesus wasn't there. They said that he had risen."

"I'd have been afraid if I'd seen an angel," said Maytwo.

"Oh, I don't know," said May. "It would be sort of special."

"I wouldn't have been afraid," Runt boasted.

May and Maytwo rolled their eyes, looked at each other, sighed, and whispered, "Embarrassing!"

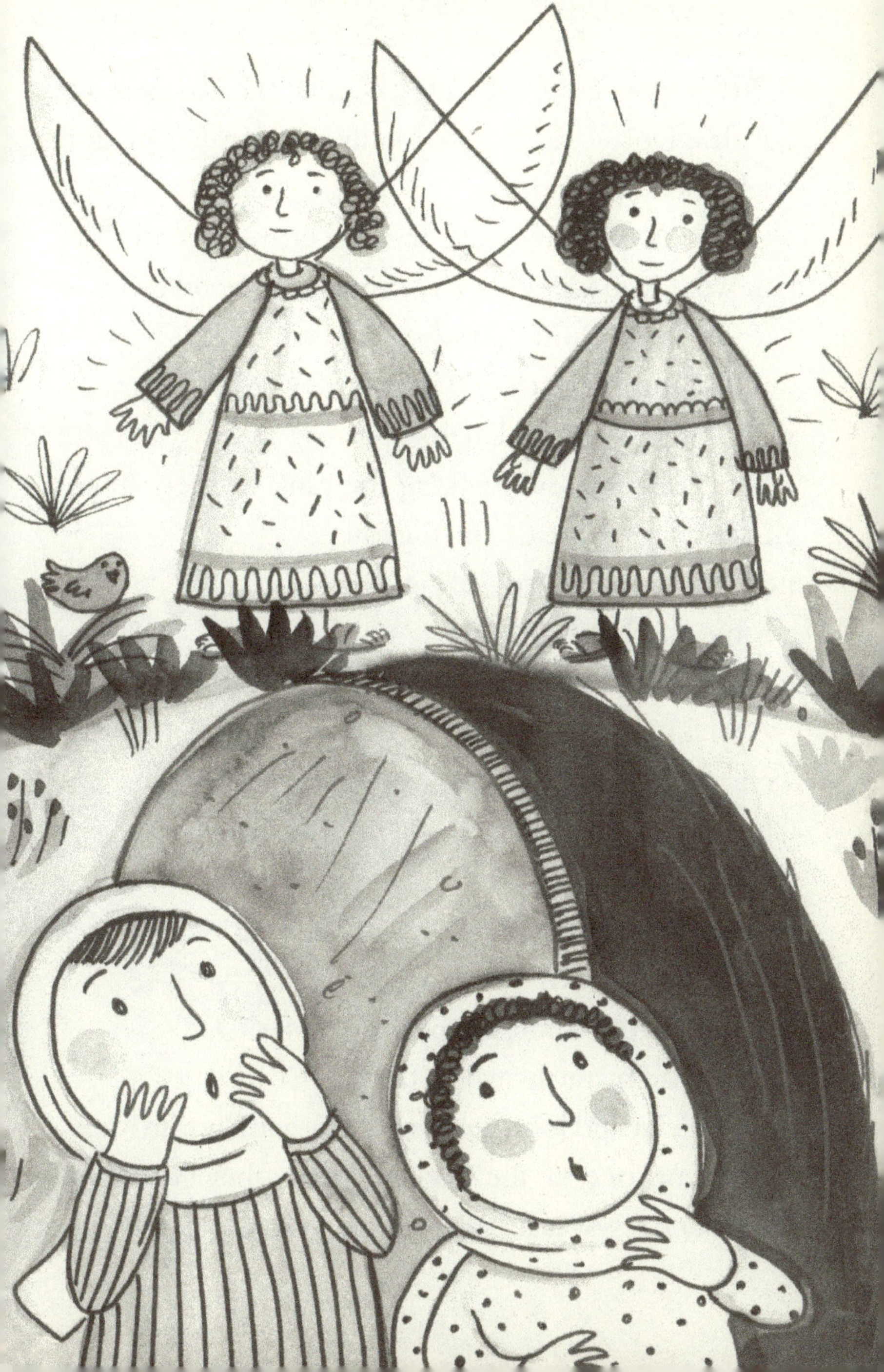

"If angels are God's messengers, what's there to be afraid of?" Runt said loudly. "Anyway, I'm not frightened of anything."

"More's the pity," said the pig farmer sourly. "If you were, you wouldn't have smashed my bike."

"Oh," said Runt. "I did say I'm sorry."

"He's proper reckless, isn't he?" said the farmer's wife. "You've got to laugh."

And that she did, making the pink feathers fly in all directions. One of the pigeons flew off the head of a gnome and landed on her hat.

"Well, the women were frightened," said Christopher Rabbit. "They ran home and told the other disciples what had happened. Some of the disciples thought the women had made the whole thing up, but Peter and John ran back to the garden with Mary Magdalene, one of the women. When they got there, they found it was just as the women had told them. The

The Empty Tomb

rock been rolled to one side of the cave entrance and there was no sign of Jesus' body. The linen cloths he had been wrapped in were neatly rolled up on the shelf where his body had lain."

"Was it still dark?" asked Nathan suddenly.

"It was probably getting light by then," said Christopher Rabbit. "Why?"

"Well, Jesus could have been hiding in the garden. He could have walked out of the tomb and hidden among the trees. You have no idea how easy it is for people to lose themselves in a garden. Mr Jubbly and I often find people wandering around the garden centre long after we've locked up."

"He couldn't have done that," said Hector scornfully. "First, he was dead when he was laid in the tomb. Second, a great rock had been rolled against the entrance. Third, there were guards on duty."

"Anyway, why would Jesus do that?" asked Christopher Rabbit.

Nathan ruffled up his crest. "So he could pretend to be the Son of God."

"But he *was* the Son of God. He didn't have to pretend," Christopher Rabbit said patiently.

"What did Peter and John do?" asked Maytwo.

Who Jesus Was

"They had a good look around, then went home. But Mary Magdalene stayed. She began to cry and turned to go. She saw a man walking toward her. Thinking he was a gardener, she ran toward him. 'Who are you looking for?' the man asked. 'If you've taken him, sir, tell me where he is,' she pleaded. The man came closer. 'Mary,' he said. Mary looked up. It was Jesus."

"Not a ghost?" asked Nathan.

The Empty Tomb

Christopher Rabbit shook his head. "Not a ghost."

Nathan thought for a moment. "Could have been a trick of the light?" he suggested.

"A trick of the light doesn't speak," Christopher Rabbit replied. "It wasn't a trick, or a ghost, or Mary's imagination. It really was Jesus, God's son, who had been raised by God from his grave and was alive, just as he had said. He told Mary to tell the other disciples that he was on his way to God, his Father, who was their Father too."

Christopher Rabbit stopped speaking.

"Well," said Nathan briskly. "I'm a plain cockerel, in a manner of speaking." He proudly puffed up his chest. "A simple bird who likes things shipshape and orderly…" He stopped to frown at the pigeons, who were laughing. "Someone who calls a spade a spade and doesn't believe what I can't see with my own eyes and touch with my own claws. It was a very good story and thank you for telling it, although I must say I don't like my garden invaded by pigs… or pigeons. But is it true? How can I believe it?"

"It is true," said Christopher Rabbit quietly. "Jesus appeared to many of his friends, including the ones who doubted – he talked with them and ate with them. Then he appeared to many other people."

"So why can't I see him?" Nathan said irritably. "Here in my garden? Not that there's much room in here for anyone else."

"We can't see him now in person, but he is still here with us in spirit," Christopher Rabbit replied. "God sent him to teach us how much God loves us – loves us so much he was willing to die for us – and to show us how to love one another."

Everyone fell silent.

"Wow!" said Whitby. "That's really amazing!"

"Does God love animals as much as humans?" Hector asked.

Christopher Rabbit considered for a moment. "God loves everything he has created, so he must love us as well," he said at last.

The pig farmer, who had sat silently on his tractor, suddenly spoke.

"I'd like to believe it, too," he said. "But I think we'd better be getting along right now. A farmer's work is never done. The pigs need feeding and this old tractor doesn't go very fast."

The Empty Tomb

"Perhaps you could buy a car?" Runt suggested eagerly. "And I could learn to…"

The farmer looked at Runt. "Don't even think about it!" he said emphatically.

May sighed. "Oh, Dad!"

"Embarrassing!" said Maytwo.

One by one the garden emptied. The pigeons flew off and Nathan, tutting at the mess they had left behind, went to get some water in order to wash the gnomes.

A leaf from a nearby tree fell, then another and another. Christopher Rabbit looked up. The trees were beginning to turn brown and gold. Autumn was coming.

"Time to go home," said Caravan Bear.

Christopher Rabbit sighed. Going home was always hard after being away in the caravan, but, he thought, brightening up, it would be fun to see his other friends.

"I'd like to know more about Jesus," said Whitby suddenly. "What sort of things did he do?"

Christopher Rabbit smiled. "I think that'll have to wait until our next adventure," he said. He picked up one of the fallen leaves.

"Thank you, God, for giving Jesus to our world, and for the wonderful things he did for us. And thank you for all the friends we've made on this trip and the adventures we've had. Give us Jesus' courage to love each other even when it's hard. And help us to know that Jesus is always beside us, wherever we are."

With that they packed up the caravan, and Hector towed it slowly out of the garden centre and on to the road home.

Nathan stood to attention at the entrance and waved goodbye with his wings. As he watched them disappear down the road, he could hear them singing.

> *"Clip clop, clip clop.*
> *Travelling fast or travelling slow,*
> *Look very hard and you might see it go:*
> *The bright caravan on the road.*
> *Clip clop, clip clop,*
> *Caravan Bear and all of his friends,*
> *Hector and Whitby, and Rabbit as well,*
> *Off for adventure, off for some fun,*
> *Off for adventure, out in the sun.*
> *Clip clop, clip clop, clip, clip clop."*

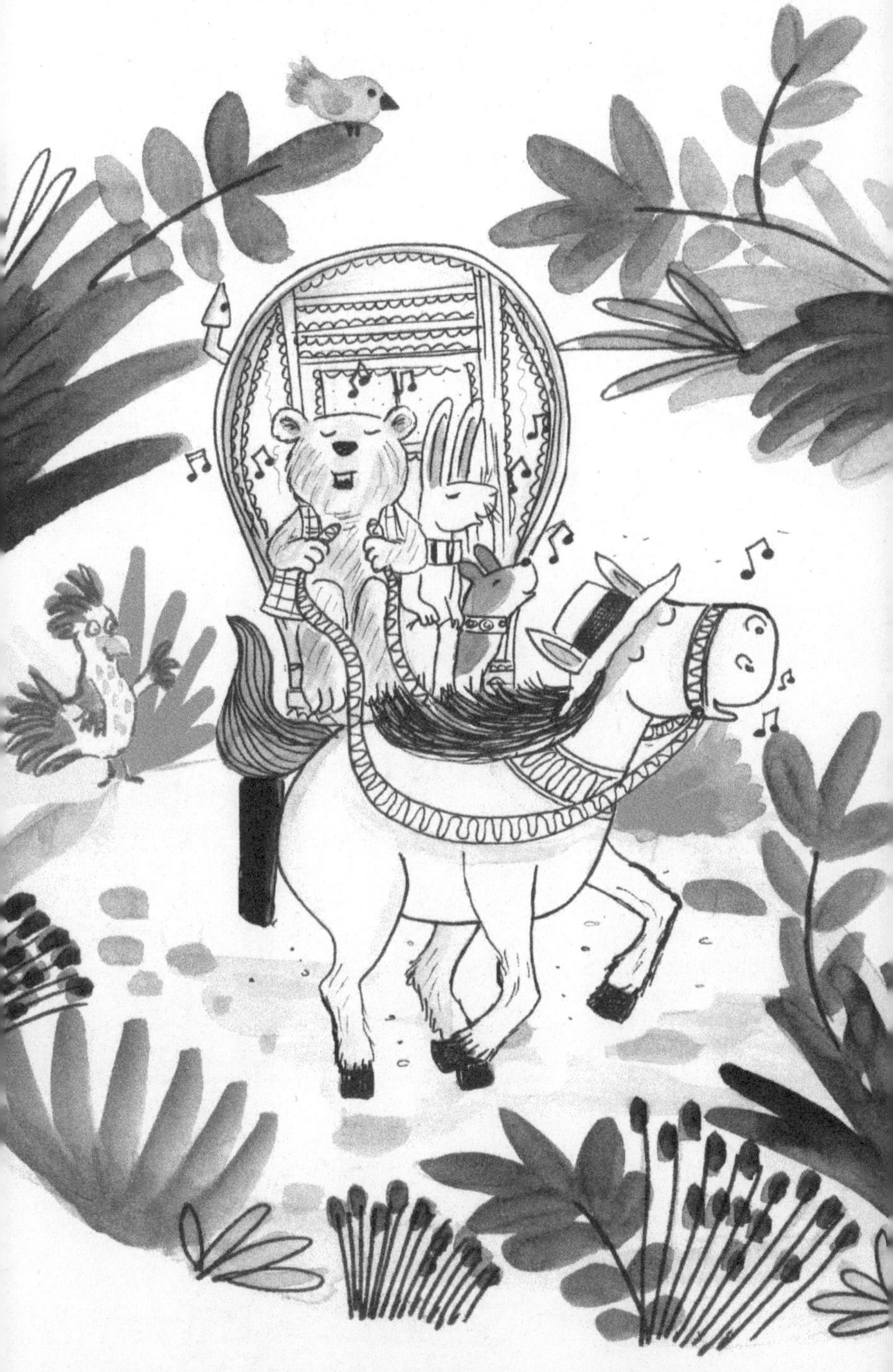

Other titles by Avril Rowlands

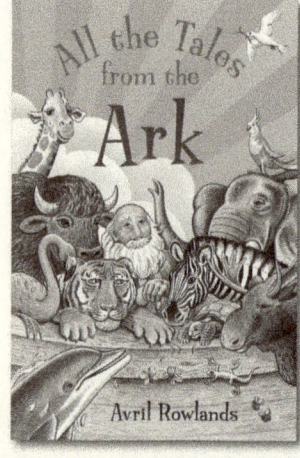

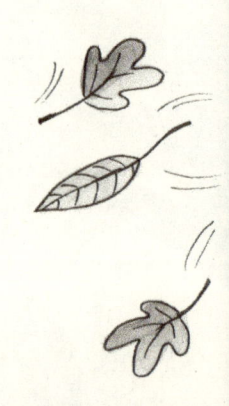

All the Tales from the Ark
Avril Rowlands

The Animals' Caravan: The Journey Begins
Avril Rowlands
Adventures through the Bible with Caravan Bear and friends

The Animals' Caravan: Stories Jesus Told
Avril Rowlands
Adventures through the Bible with Caravan Bear and friends

The Animals' Caravan: The Journey Continues
Avril Rowlands
Adventures through the Bible with Caravan Bear and friends